MW00678251

FIRST EDITION

INFORMED TEACHING

USING DATA TO IMPROVE EDUCATIONAL PERFORMANCE

DR. MICHAEL S. MOTT, DR. DENISE A. SOARES,
AND DR. SUSAN S. MCCLELLAND

Bassim Hamadeh, CEO and Publisher
Jennifer McCarthy, Acquisitions Editor
Gem Rabanera, Project Editor
Christian Berk, Associate Production Editor
Miguel Macias, Senior Graphic Designer
Alexa Lucido, Licensing Coordinator
Natalie Piccotti, Senior Marketing Manager
Kassie Graves, Director of Acquisitions and Sales
Jamie Giganti, Senior Managing Editor

Cover image: Copyright © 2016 iStockphoto LP/Rogotanie.

Printed in the United States of America.

ISBN: 978-1-5165-2866-0 (pbk) / 978-1-5165-2867-7 (br)

INFORMED TEACHING

USING DATA TO IMPROVE EDUCATIONAL PERFORMANCE

CONTENTS

ASSESSMENT EXAMPLE 1. ASSESSMENT OF PHONOLOGICAL AND MORPHOLOGICAL AWARENESS **42**

ASSESSMENT EXAMPLE 8. NORM-REFERENCE ACHIEVEMENT TEST DATA   202

INTRODUCTION

Informed Teaching: Using Data to Improve Educational Performance is a book for professional educators, agency professionals involved in teaching and training, and students learning how to teach in school environments. Informed Teaching is recommended reading for those learning methods for measuring learner performance across content areas and social-emotional development for purposes of instructional decision making and predictive, diagnostic, and evaluative purposes. The complexity of assessment, including testing, measuring, evaluating, and predicting for making formative and summative instructional judgments, is addressed using a validity framework for understanding what characteristics an assessment purports to contain that support learning objectives and goals. Several assessment examples are articulated in this book, and the reader will use an "interactive map" to identify characteristics of the examples and make connections about how the example assessments can improve the teaching and learning process in content areas and social-emotionally across age and grade levels. Reliability, validity, value, and utility in assessment will be explained as a framework for how educators can make inferences from data with confidence and alignment to the intended purpose of an assessment. The following examples of assessment are used for the reader to "interact" with; some contain background research and information as well as sample items/prompts, and they represent a wide array of developmental learning levels, content, and both cognitive and affective domains. The following list outlines the sample assessments used in this book for understanding a wide range of type, characteristic, and purpose:

Literacy Emergent Skills for K–5 Mainstream and K–12 Special Education Students

1   Assessment of Phonological and Morphological Awareness

2   Phonics Inventory Sample

Assessment examples 1 and 2 consist of literacy subareas of phonological awareness (sound discrimination), morphological awareness (smallest meaningful units of words) and decoding (sound–symbol correspondence, commonly referred to as "alphabetics") for a wide developmental range of learning related to reading and learning how to read.

Spelling Development for K–8

3   Developmental Spelling Inventory Sample

Assessment example 3, the Developmental Spelling Inventory Sample, supports teachers by providing an understanding of how children in grades K–8 and K–12 with special needs spell words so that specific areas of word structure can be focused on for instruction.

Writing (Narrative)

4   Narrative Writing Rubric for Media (WWYR)

Assessment example 4, the WWYR, enables teachers to evaluate K–12 student narratives (stories) along analytic components of narrative genre. Teachers can facilitate student understanding along theme, plot, setting, character, and communication, explicitly interacting with students about goals involved in each component and in juxtaposition to their personal creative written story.

Literacy Reading Subareas

5   Oral Reading Fluency Sample

Example 5, Oral Reading Fluency (ORF), is a key index of reading comprehension, which is the reason for and end goal of reading. ORF measures three key aspects of reading: (1) speed, as measured in words read per minute; (2) accuracy; and (3) expression, or the degree to which the reader uses variance in pitch and tone to accentuate story and character with social-emotional underpinnings.

Science Process and Content

6   Media-Enhanced Science Presentation Rubric (MESPR)

The MESPR assessment example addresses student learning in the content area of science and addresses communication skills involved with sharing the results of scientific experiments.

Classroom Behavior and Management

7   Classroom Management Survey Sample

An observation and recording chart with defined criteria for behavior related to classroom management is articulated, allowing assessment example 7 to address the affective versus cognitive domains in teaching and learning.

Achievement Test for Comparing Scores in a Large Population

8   Norm-Reference Achievement Test Data

Test objectives, item examples, and a hypothetical-results printout delineating student scores is used in assessment example 8 to demonstrate overall purposes and goals of a large-scale norm-reference standardized reading test for high school.

CHALLENGES OF TEACHING AND LEARNING

Educational settings are influenced by the increasing intellectual and cultural desire to measure performance along a standard or set of standards for meeting learning goals and objectives, certification requirements, authentication of a training, graduation, and criteria-based acceptance or denial. Our society contains a sense of fairness and equity related to how we are to manage those learning in an ethical manner. Likewise, we wish to function as guardians and mediators of promotion for professions, certifications, graduations, grade-level promotions, and all kinds of consent or denial for educational promotion, minute by minute, day to day, month to month, and end of year. Thus a tall order is placed upon assessments used by educators, as a wide array of learning needs require testing, measurement, prediction, and evaluation. "Assessment" in this book is used as the umbrella term that covers all of these needs but can refer to a single assessment (for example, of learning how to write a narrative or a process of assessment involving a multipronged approach for evaluating the effectiveness of the early literacy curriculum employed in first grade). This book will focus on assessment to improve teaching and learning across age and grade levels K–8.

ASSESSMENT FOR INFORMING TEACHING AND LEARNING

In all educational settings, there is a need for an understanding of what to teach and when and ultimately to find out if, or to what degree, learning has taken place. A **test** is used to determine what someone has learned, while **evaluation** provides us the ability to make judgements about a person or program. **Measurement** enables educators to see how much someone has learned. **Assessment** is the connective term for all three and functions to both differentiate and bridge. The complexity of assessment, in not only the varying types defined above, lies in the myriad and multiple purposes of their intended use. For example, a classroom behavioral observation checklist assessment is designed to inform the teacher about when certain behaviors take place and in what context so that she can anticipate behavior, a key to classroom management. Juxtapose this social-emotional assessment with the statewide reading achievement test, which is designed to measure student ability in reading and compare scores across the entire state to inform educational policy makers about the effectiveness of large-scale budgeted programming and curriculum initiatives.

The two above assessment examples, one a mere classroom checklist and the other a large-scale achievement test, contain similar and different purposes. They both are intended to improve learning generally. Specifically, however, they are different in that the classroom assessment, which enables the teacher to chart behavior minute by minute, informs her

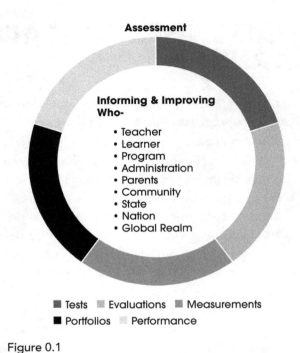

Assessment

Informing & Improving Who-

- Teacher
- Learner
- Program
- Administration
- Parents
- Community
- State
- Nation
- Global Realm

■ Tests   ▦ Evaluations   ■ Measurements
■ Portfolios   ▦ Performance

Figure 0.1

Behavior Observation Checklist Charting Assessment

instructional decision making immediately. She is not gauging cognitive ability but is working to improve classroom management, which is an important precondition to learning. She is not measuring cognition, "thinking," or achievement from an academic sense. The achievement test, let's hypothetically say, measures statewide eighth-grade reading levels and specifically compares student scores in reading comprehension based upon their response to literature passages. Scores, or test data, can then be analyzed by state education policy leaders, superintendents, principals, teachers, parents, and other community members. The purpose of the test is not to directly inform teachers what to teach in terms of reading comprehension, but it does provide information about their students' general performance compared to the rest of the state. Assessment example 6, which you will read about later in this book, provides the teacher immediate information on a student's understandings and misunderstandings of a passage, leading to immediate teacher instructional intervention. Unlike Assessment example 6, our achievement test does not lead to immediate classroom intervention but does contain invaluable information about the general ability of a student or group of students so that decisions can be made on a large scale about curriculum, materials, funding, and other leadership directives.

Note that we can see from these two drastically different assessments that the intended purpose of an assessment is predicated upon the validity, or its intended purpose. Validity is the degree to which an assessment measures what it purports to measure. The validity of an assessment can vary greatly. Figure 0.1, the behavior observation checklist charting assessment, is valid for making inferences from the results about anticipating student behavior in context, whereas the statewide reading achievement test is valid for comparing student reading comprehension scores across the state. In order to understand the complexity of assessment so that you can make appropriate inferences from assessment data, it is thus necessary to understand validity and other technical characteristics of assessments.

Validity: Measures what is supposed to be measure

COLLECTING AND USING FORMATIVE AND SUMMATIVE STUDENT ASSESSMENT DATA

In today's educational environment, principals and teachers have access to more data in multiple forms than ever before. With the passage of No Child Left Behind (NCLB) in 2002 and the Every Student Succeeds Act (ESSA) in 2015, educators operate in an era of educational accountability and school improvement. With greater emphasis on accountability, educators are required to monitor student performance using multiple sources of data. These data may include summative assessments (high-stakes tests), formative assessments, and demographic data as well as informal classroom observations. Access to various forms of data allows teachers to monitor student performance closely and make informed decisions regarding the instructional needs of their students. As a result, data-driven decision making has become an emerging practice for educators.

INTRODUCTION TO DATA-DRIVEN DECISION MAKING

Data-driven decision making (DDDM) is the systematic collection, analysis, examination, interpretation, and use of multiple forms of data from a variety of sources to inform teacher practice and improve student performance (Choppin 2002; Mandinach 2012; Marsh, Pane, and Hamilton 2006, cited in Schifter et al. 2014). While policy makers have considered DDDM as a system primarily for accountability, at the classroom level, DDDM is a "learner-centered teaching tool that supports differentiated instruction by providing information that helps teachers tailor instruction to fit class and individual learning needs" (Dunn, Airola, Lo, and Garrison 2013). Teachers who apply DDDM with fidelity examine their classroom decision making, selection of materials used in the classroom, and the manner in which the materials are presented to better align their instructional strategies to meet the learning needs of their students (Dunn, Airola, Lo, and Garrison 2013; Murray 2014). Luo (2008) further supports the ideals of DDDM as an "interactive, multifaceted, and contextual practice within the school organization" (p. 610).

DDDM is a sophisticated system, as it requires teachers to clearly understand the dichotomy between declarative knowledge (knowing what) and procedural knowledge (knowing how). Declarative knowledge answers the question "What do you know?" In classroom instruction, declarative knowledge provides information regarding who, what, when, and where. Marzano defines this knowledge as "informational in nature" (Marzano 2007, p. 60). For example, teachers may ask students to identify the main character in a story, write the definitions of spelling words, write a personal narrative, or identify significant historical events. Teachers

declarative knowledge: Knowing information

assess declarative knowledge by having students take spelling tests, write a book report, or describe a process like building a snowman. We see declarative knowledge assessments given routinely in today's classrooms through traditional assessment forms. In contrast, procedural knowledge answers the question "What can you do?" Procedural knowledge is demonstrated: it is the student's ability to carry out actions to complete a task. For example, a teacher may ask a student to compare and contrast two stories, to act out a scene of a play, to build a replica of an atom and explain the process, or to compose a haiku. Procedural knowledge assignment instructions use verbs, and the verbs used will determine the cognitive levels at which the students will work. Consider a third-grade College and Career Readiness Standard for English Language Arts: "CCR.R.9: Analyze how two or more texts address similar themes or topics in order to build knowledge or to compare the approaches the authors take" (CCSS 2010). Within this standard, students are asked to identify important points within multiple texts, identify supporting details in multiple texts, and compare/contrast (orally or in writing) the most important points within multiple texts. Because students are asked to "compare" and "contrast" using two or more texts, the level of difficulty is more complex, and students are operating at the analysis level of higher-order thinking. Procedural knowledge is more complex and requires students to think and work at deeper levels.

ASSESSMENTS OF AND FOR LEARNING

According to Ellen Mandinach (2012), policy makers and educational administrators have traditionally relied on data based primarily on assessments *of* learning that measure what students learn, much like declarative knowledge. Often these data don't match the standards of the existing curricula and are difficult to adapt to classroom instructional goals (Stecher and Hamilton 2006). However, "assessments *for* learning have begun to take hold because of their ability to provide data that can help to improve teaching and student learning" (Mandinach, p. 82). Assessments *for* learning are intended to assist teachers in adjusting instruction that leads to increased student achievement. Educators often refer to assessment *for* learning as formative assessments. These assessments are taken periodically throughout the academic year and are intended to inform practice to lead to increased student achievement. The trend toward the use of formative assessments in the classroom should decrease the disconnect between state assessments, which assess primarily declarative knowledge, and instructional standards as well as the continual growth of students (Stecher and Hamilton 2006).

PEDAGOGICAL DATA LITERACY

instruction decision making

Individuals typically become educators because they have a desire to educate children, to make a difference in the world, to create a more literate society. Individuals typically don't major in education to be statisticians or to spend hours reviewing data. For many educators,

"Data, in and of themselves, are meaningless. They are simply numbers. Data gain meaning through context" (Mandinach, p. 73). And data tend to gain meaning for educators when they represent the needs, challenges, and successes of students. Effective teachers translate the meaning of data into "actions that inform instruction." This transference of data to instructional action is called *pedagogical data literacy* (p. 73) or *instructional decision making* (Means et al. 2011). Pedagogical data literacy refers to the teacher's ability to transform the numbers and statistics into instructional strategies that meet the needs of specific students (Mandinach, p. 76). Consider the following scenario: a third-grade reading teacher examines classroom data that shows many of her students haven't mastered the College

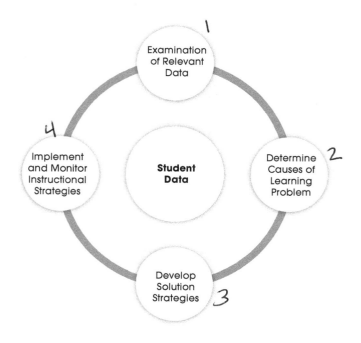

Figure 0.2

Implementing this thoughtful process demonstrates a teacher's pedagogical data literacy—the ability to transform formative assessment data into instructional strategies to meet the specific learning needs of individual students.

and Career Readiness Standard CCR.R.2, which asks that students "Determine central ideas or themes of a text and analyze their development; summarize the key supporting details and ideas." Specifically, they are struggling with the performance indicator: students should provide a statement of the central message, lesson, or moral in a text. After reviewing the student data carefully, the teacher looks for patterns or reasons why the students responded incorrectly. Once she has determined where students' understandings have faltered, she designs instructional strategies to reteach the standard and remediate students' learning. She carefully monitors the students' performance to determine if the remediation is appropriate for each student's needs. Love, Stiles, Mundry, and DiRanna (2008) describe the teacher's process in the following way: (1) examine relevant data to identify a student learning problem, (2) determine the causes of the learning problem, (3) develop solution strategies, and (4) implement and monitor alternate instructional strategies (see Figure 0.2).

THE INTERACTIVE ASSESSMENT WORK-MAP

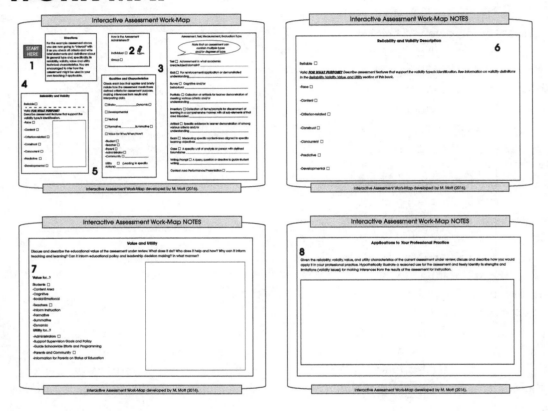

Figure 0.3

HOW TO USE THE INTERACTIVE ASSESSMENT WORK-MAP

In order to better understand assessment characteristics along reliability, validity, value, and utility, you will "engage" the sample assessment via the Interactive Assessment Work-Map (Figure 0.3). There are eight steps to completing the work-map for each assessment example in the book.

Step 1 prompts you to "interact" with the assessment under review. Note that you should read and review the sections in this book addressing reliability, validity, value, and utility, and pay close attention to the front matter describing the assessment, such as directions, background, research rationalizing the design of it, and the connection it contains to curriculum and instructional methodology.

interact

Step 2 requests information on how the assessment is administered. Is the assessment administered to the entire class or to an individual only? Might you be able to administer it to a small group for differentiation of instruction? This is important, especially as it relates to value for the classroom. If an assessment can be group administered, time is preserved for the teacher, as the assessment can occur in a narrow time frame, versus an individually administered assessment, which may take much longer as students rotate through the teacher for assessment.

how it is administered

Step 3 solicits information on assessment type. For example, is the sample assessment an inventory that deals with specific aspects of the curriculum or psychological construct? The assessment might be in the form of a published and norm-referenced achievement exam or a teacher-made quiz for responding to literature. The important part of Step 3 is to identify the type and then reflect on how the type relates to the curriculum goals and learning objectives at hand.

Assessment Type

Step 4 seeks the identification of assessment features for reliability and validity by type(s) of validity. Note that you may see multiple validity types for a single assessment. What is important about making sense of the validity of an assessment is that once you accurately do so you are able to then understand how to make inferences from assessment data and results. You can then appropriately qualify what results mean for a given learning scenario, individual, or groups of students. This will also enable you to use the assessment correctly to aid you in determining what your students actually need to learn, based upon assessment results in a particular learning content area or psychological domain.

determine what students need to learn

Steps 5 (generally) and 7 (specifically) involve additional information for the sample assessment value and utility. Is the assessment a one-shot deal, or does it involve use in the middle of a learning session to guide next steps? Is it formative, summative, or both? Note that with many of these categories, they are not mutually exclusive, and certain examples will contain qualities across categories. Lastly, what do the results mean, and for who do they mean something? The teacher? Principal? Superintendent? Student or parent? The governor's office, etc.?

Assessment value + utility

Step 6 requires you to narratively describe the validity qualities of the sample assessment. Again, certain assessments may contain numerous validity characteristics, and this has repercussions for how educators should use assessment results to improve student performance. It is advisable to use the research, background, or direction information provided for some of the sample assessments to better understand validity.

Lastly, in Step 8, you will describe how you might apply (theoretically/hypothetically or in reality if your classroom instruction might benefit from using the assessment) the sample assessment to your instruction and connect how assessment results will aid your understanding of whether or to what degree students are meeting educational objectives.

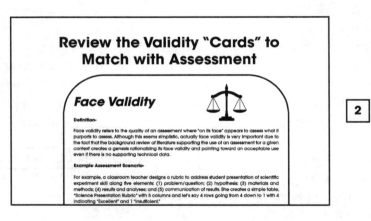

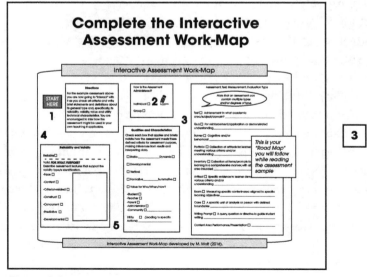

Figure 0.4

Interact with the Assessment Process

Interactive Assessment Work-Map

Directions

For the example assessment above you are now going to "interact" with it as you check off criteria and write brief statements and definitions about its general type and, specifically, its reliability, validity, value and utility technical characteristics. You are encouraged to infer how the assessment might be used in your own teaching if applicable.

1

4

How Is the Assessment Administered?

2

Individual ☐

Group ☐

3

Assessment, Test, Measurement, Evaluation Type

Note that an assessment can contain multiple types and/or degrees of type.

Test ☐ Achievement in what academic area/subject/domain?

Quiz ☐ For reinforcement/applicaiton or demonstrated understanding _____

Survey ☐ Cognitive and/or behavioral

Portfolio ☐ Collection of artifacts for learner meeting various criteria and/or understan

Inventory ☐ Collection of items/prompts fo learning in a comprehensive manner, with all area included _____

Artifact ☐ Specific evidence to learner dem various criteria and/or understanding

Exam ☐ Measuring specific content-area aligned to specific learning objectives _____

Case ☐ A specific unit of analysis or person with defined boundaries _____

Writing Prompt ☐ A query, question or directive to guide student writing _____

Content Area Performance/Presentation ☐ _____

This is your "Road Map" you will follow while reading the assessment sample

Qualities and Characteristics

Check each box that applies and briefly notate how the assessment meets these defined criteria for assessment purpose, making inferences from results and interpreting data.

☐ Static-_____Dynamic ☐

☐ Developmental

☐ Vertical

☐ Formative_____Summative ☐

☐ Value for Who/When/How?

-Student ☐
-Teacher ☐
-Parent ☐
-Administrator ☐
-Community ☐ _____

Utility ☐ (Leading to specific Actions) _____

5

Reliability and Validity

Reliable ☐

Valid **FOR WHAT PURPOSE?**
Describe assessment features that support the validity type/s identification.

-Face ☐

-Content ☐

-Criterion-related ☐

-Construct ☐

-Concurrent ☐

-Predictive ☐

-Developmental ☐

Interactive Assessment Work-Map developed by M. Mott (2016).

Figure 0.5

Interactive Assessment Work-Map NOTES

Reliability and Validity Description

6

Reliable ☐

Valid **FOR WHAT PURPOSE?** *Describe assessment features that support the validity type/s identification. See information on validity definitions in the Reliability, Validity, Value, and Utility section of this book.*

-Face ☐

-Content ☐

-Criterion-related ☐

-Construct ☐

-Concurrent ☐

-Predictive ☐

-Developmental ☐

As you use your "Cards" take notes here while comprehending the assessment samples text

Interactive Assessment Work-Map developed by M. Mott (2016).

Figure 0.6

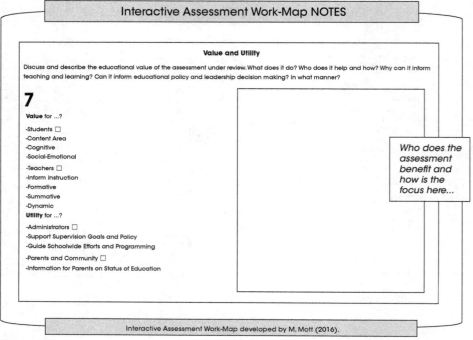

Figure 0.7

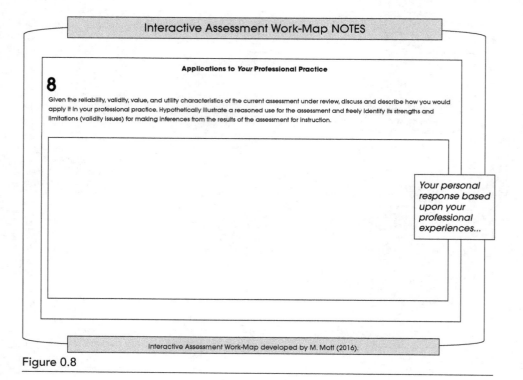

Figure 0.8

CURRENT RESEARCH ON ASSESSMENT TESTING, MEASUREMENT, EVALUATION, AND ASSESSMENT

Testing, measurement, evaluation, and assessment are terms that all revolve around similar topics, but they each have varied meanings. A test is used to examine someone's knowledge of something—to determine what he or she knows or has learned as determined by educational goals and objectives. An evaluation is the process of making judgments based on preconceived criteria and evidence for assigning value to a program or even a single piece of work such as a writing sample. Assessment is the overarching and holistic process of documenting knowledge, skills, attitudes, and beliefs, usually in a measurable format. The goal of assessment is to guide instructional decision making minute by minute and day by day, as opposed to simply producing judgements or scores.

evaluation: making judgments

In a purely educational context, assessment is the process of describing, collecting, recording, scoring, and interpreting information about learning to inform instruction and also to increase student metacognition. Measurement is used when asking "how much" (for example, asking how much is left to learn, how much a particular student has learned, and how much more time should be spent on this objective). Measurement is a process involving both theoretical and empirical considerations. "Measurement focuses on the crucial relationship between the empirically grounded indicators—that is, the observable response—and the underlying unobservable concepts" (Carmines 1979, p. 11).

To summarize, we give forms of assessment (tests, ratings, rubrics, checklists, quizzes, portfolios, etc.) to students, and we evaluate results in terms of some set of criteria. Thus, assessment, testing, measurement, and evaluation are inextricably connected, intertwined, and nonexclusive to each other but do contain differences under certain conditions related to their validity. It is useful to think of them as separate but connected ideas and processes and, most importantly, to understand how to make inferences from the data they yield according to their intended purpose (validity).

RELIABILITY, VALIDITY, VALUE, AND UTILITY "CARDS" FOR COMPLETING THE INTERACTIVE ASSESSMENT WORK-MAP

In order to use the Interactive Assessment Work-Map, while working to better understand your sample assessment, you will use the "Cards" in the next section of this book to match assessment characteristics with the sample. Note that there are not necessarily "right" answers!

Some assessment examples might contain validity, value, or utility characteristics across numerous categories, with perhaps one or two traits being more prolific than others. Thus, keep an open mind, especially about validity. Validity enables the educator to make inferences from results: for example, what kinds of inferences can be made for who, what, when, and how can we move forward (or backward, for differentiated learning across ability and developmental levels), based upon the results?

THE CONCEPT AND HIERARCHY OF VALIDITY

Meaningful & Appropriate

Validity refers to the degree or extent to which inferences from results are meaningful and appropriate. There are numerous types of validity of varying technical qualities, and, according to Messick (1989), assessment designers strive to achieve the highest level of validity, but true and perfect validity is not possible. We merely "reach" for perfect validity. Thus there exists a hierarchy of validity, with "face" validity being an initial lower type not requiring anything more than answering the question "does the assessment, on its face, appear valid?" Juxtapose this with a more stringent and difficult-to-achieve validity like predictive validity, which refers to an assessments quality of yielding results that enable one to make inferences for predicting the ability of individuals or groups to excel in a given context. The following section outlines each validity type, but, again, it is very important to note that ultimately we only strive to have the highest degree validity, but we cannot have perfect validity, and note that one assessment may contain numerous validity types.

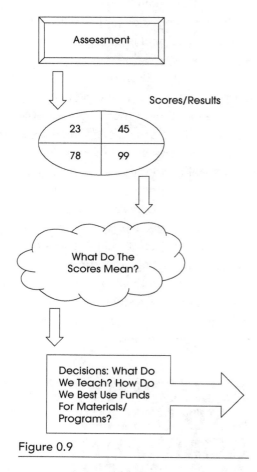

Figure 0.9

The hierarchy of validity (see Figure 0.9) deals with how assessments are validated and the nature of how an assessment is to be used. For example, with face validity, an assessment might be rationalized based upon an extensive review of literature rationalizing its use for a given context, such as an analytic writing rubric, based upon how proficient writers attain high quality as revealed in the research literature. Conversely, for predictive validity, advanced

Face Validity

Definition-

Face validity refers to the quality of an assessment where "on its face" appears to assess what it purports to assess. Although this seems simplistic, actually face validity is very important due to the fact that the background review of literature supporting the use of an assessment for a given context creates a genesis rationalizing its face validity and pointing toward an acceptable use even if there is no supporting technical data.

Example Assessment Scenario-

For example, a classroom teacher designs a rubric to address student presentation of scientific experiment skill along five elements: (1) problem/question; (2) hypothesis; (3) materials and methods; (4) results and analyses; and (5) communication of results. She creates a simple table, "Science Presentation Rubric" with 5 columns and let's say 4 rows going from 4 down to 1 with 4 indicating "Excellent" and 1 "Insufficient."

Inside the table cells of the five column scientific elements by four rows/levels of academic proficiency of science experiment presentation the teacher places text describing what is necessary for the student to meet that expectation of presentation. The face validity of this example would be based upon the research-based use of the scientific method advocated by The American Association for the Advancement of Science, the National Science Teacher Association and Project 2061 body of research highlighting the need for K–12 students to engage in the scientific method to learn science and raise science literacy. Since the teacher made rubric hypothetically consists of the scientific method and method steps are accurately described in the rubric we can conclude that use of this assessment is valid for interpreting the results to assess student knowledge of the scientific method and their ability to articulate and communicate experiment results.

Research Addressing Face Validity-

Face validity precedes construct validity as an important step towards validating an instrument.

Morlini, I., Stella, G., and Scorza, M. (2015). Assessing Decoding Ability: The Role of Speed and Accuracy and a New Composite Indicator to Measure Decoding Skill in Elementary Grades. *Journal of Learning Disabilities*, 48(2), 176–195 20p. doi:10.1177/0022219413495298.

Figure 0.10

statistical analysis is applied to the scores of test takers to determine the degree to which high, medium, or low scores are related to high, medium, or low achievement in a given context such as college academics. You will see, in the sections of assessment samples and scenarios in this book, that for different validity types there are different ways to validate an instrument and different contexts for the validity types one can make inferences from.

"CARDS" FOR ANALYZING ASSESSMENT QUALITIES

For each assessment example, sample assessment, or scenario outlined in the various content areas in this book, you will use "Validity Cards" to analyze the assessment along basic definition, scenario, and recent research (Figures 0.11–0.20). Several of the assessments contain background research, and all of them have an accompanying rationale and/or a set of directions for appropriate use. Note that a given assessment may have multiple validity types that can be attributed to inferences from scores, descriptions, checks, or ratings.

Face Validity

Definition-

Face validity refers to the quality of an assessment where "on its face" appears to assess what it purports to assess. Although this seems simplistic, actually face validity is very important due to the fact that the background review of literature supporting the use of an assessment for a given context creates a genesis rationalizing its face validity and pointing toward an acceptable use even if there is no supporting technical data.

Example Assessment Scenario-

For example, a classroom teacher designs a rubric to address student presentation of scientific experiment skill along five elements: (1) problem/question; (2) hypothesis; (3) materials and methods; (4) results and analyses; and (5) communication of results. She creates a simple table, "Science Presentation Rubric" with 5 columns and let's say 4 rows going from 4 down to 1 with 4 indicating "Excellent" and 1 "Insufficient."

Inside the table cells of the five column scientific elements by four rows/levels of academic proficiency of science experiment presentation the teacher places text describing what is necessary for the student to meet that expectation of presentation. The face validity of this example would be based upon the research-based use of the scientific method advocated by The American Association for the Advancement of Science, the National Science Teacher Association and Project 2061 body of research highlighting the need for K-12 students to engage in the scientific method to learn science and raise science literacy. Since the teacher made rubric hypothetically consists of the scientific method and method steps are accurately described in the rubric we can conclude that use of this assessment is valid for interpreting the results to assess student knowledge of the scientific method and their ability to articulate and communicate experiment results.

Research Addressing Face Validity-

Face validity precedes construct validity as an important step towards validating an instrument.

Morlini, I., Stella, G., and Scorza, M. (2015). Assessing Decoding Ability: The Role of Speed and Accuracy and a New Composite Indicator to Measure Decoding Skill in Elementary Grades. *Journal of Learning Disabilities*, 48(2), 176–195 20p. doi:10.1177/0022219413495298.

Figure 0.11

Content Validity

Definition-

Content validity is the degree to which assessment results can be used to determine performance along a specified content area it purports to assess. For example a rubric designed to measure students' science process skills related to the scientific method of experimentation is used to guide student communication of experiment results.

Example Assessment Scenario-

For example a rubric designed to measure students' science process skills related to the scientific method of experimentation is used to guide student communication of experiment results. Within the science content area a teacher can discern the degree to which her students are mastering the components of an experiment based upon their communication of experiment results along hypothesis; method; data collection; analysis; and results categories. The content being assessed is the scientific method and the process skills of designing, conducting and communicating experiment results with text, graphics and visual information. See the section in this book "Media Enhanced Science Presentation Rubric (MESPR)."

Research Addressing Content Validity-

A measure of reading achievement embedded in an instructional approach is addressed by McCane and the content of learning how to read strategically for comprehension is the focus.

McCane-Bowling, S. E. (2014). The Utility of Maze Accurate Resonse Rate in Assessing Reading Comprehension in Upper Elementary Students and Middle School Students. *Psychology In The Schools*, 51(8), 789–800.

In all three examples below a rubric is used to align teacher feedback to students along educational objectives-language located in the columns and rows of the instrument.

Mott, M.S., Chessin, D., Sumrall, W.J., Rutherford, A.S., and Moore, V.J. (2011). Assessing student scientific expression using media: The MESPR-Media enhanced science presentation rubric. *Journal of STEM Education: Innovations & Research*, 12(1).

Sumrall, W.J., and Mott, M.S. (2010). Building models to better understand cost versus safety in engineering. *Science Scope*, 35(2), 45–52.

Mott, M.S., Etsler, C., and Drumgold, D. (2003). Applying an analytic writing rubric to children's hypermedia narratives. *Early Childhood Research & Practice*, (5)1. (Online).

Figure 0.12

Criterion-Related Validity

Definition-

Criterion-related validity is the degree to which assessment performance scores are related (correlated) to a predefined criteria or outcome. The criteria or outcome might be scores positively related to: grade point average; low dropout rate; graduation; IQ, etc. See the table below to see how criterion-related validity differs from other validity types where norm reference is involved.

Assessment Quality	Criterion-Related	Norm-Referenced
Purpose	To assess achievement along specified skill on content area concepts. To discern student knowledge prior to and after instruction.	To rank an individual along a broad area of learning. To level learners from low to high performing.
Content	Assess specific skills in a curriculum. Skills assessed are identified via assessment objectives.	Assess broad skill areas from learning over time and from interacting with an assortment of materials.
Item/Prompts	Each skill related to the criteria that is tested is evaluated at least 4 times to ensure that items align with the skill and items are made to equivalence of difficulty.	Items are not equivalent along difficulty.
Making Inferences from Scores	Assessment scores are compared to the predefined levels of acceptable achievement or outcomes. The scores of others are not relevant as the score is only compared against the criteria via percentage.	Each score is compared to the scores of others versus a comparison of individual to specific skill.

Example Assessment Scenario-

A long division test is designed to see the degree to which student achievement along the subcomponent of division, a math computation skill, to determine mastery or achievement level of the test taker.

Research Addressing Criterion-related Validity-

Ganske, K. (1999). The Developmental Spelling Analysis: A Measure of Orthographic Knowledge. *Educational Assessment*, 6(1), 41.

Figure 0.13

Construct Validity

Definition-

Construct validity is the degree to which an assessment measures or assists in defining a single domain it purports to assess. A construct consists of one domain such as "depression" in the field of psychology or "phonological processing" ability in K–3 children in early childhood education or "obesity" in medical science. Can an assessment reveal a single construct/unidimensional domain or do depression, phonological processing and obesity actually consist of many domains/ components/variables/sources?

Example Assessment Scenario-

In the Literacy assessment section of this book see the Early Literacy Assessment (ELA) example. For young children to learn to read they begin with sound discrimination since eventually they will have to engage in matching sounds to corresponding letters in phonics and beginning word identification. Mott and Rutherford wanted to know could the ELA identify children's sound discrimination, or phonological awareness, 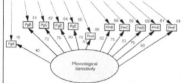 as consisting of a single unidimensional construct? Although there 11 basic levels of are phonological ability, the answer is yes, phonological awareness is a unidimensional construct. All 11 levels of sound discrimination are indeed related to this idea (construct) of "phonological processing." Typically when structural equation modelling (SEM) is used, the construct will be represented by a bubble with variables connected depicting correlational coefficients or relatedness of the variables to the construct. In this case, all 11 sound discrimination levels were highly related to phonological processing in children K–3.

Research Addressing Construct Validity-

The following citation consists of the full study summarized above.

Mott, M.S., and Rutherford, A.S. (2012). Technical examination of a measure of phonological sensitivity. *Sage Open*: http://sgo.sagepub.com/.

Figure 0.14

Predictive Validity

Definition-

Predictive validity is the degree to which an assessment scores or ratings predict performance or tendencies in the future.

Example Assessment Scenario-

The STAR assessment for 3rd grade reading achievement provides norm referenced scores enabling an individual to be compared to the population taking the test along the content area of reading achievement. If the STAR contains predictive validity, an individual with a high score in reading achievement in 3rd grade would excel with high performance in the 4th grade reading curriculum. Likewise, a college entrance exam, or interview process with ratings based upon interviewee responses, might contain predictive ability for success in academics in college across the curriculum.

Research Addressing Predictive Validity-

The following citation is a research study on the predictive validity of a reading measure.

McCane-Bowling, S. E. (2014). The Utility of Maze Accurate Resonse Rate in Assessing Reading Comprehension in Upper Elementary Students and Middle School Students. *Psychology In The Schools*, 51(8), 789–800.

Figure 0.15

Developmental Validity

Definition-

Developmental validity of a measure is the degree to which scores or ratings have the sensitivity to reveal a developmental progression or continuum.

Example Assessment Scenario-

The Writing What You Read (WWYR) rubric (Wolf, 1995) was designed to measure quality of students' narrative writing along five components: (1) plot; (2) setting; (3) theme; (4) character and (5) communication. A five year old writes, with inventive spelling, a story: The bad guy went to the zoo (D BD GI WT T D ZU). Next page: The zebra was friendly (D ZBR WZ FLE). Along plot, the first level of the rubric would indicate "one or two list like statements" indicating that the teachers' feedback should consist of language teaching plot and storyline development of beginning, middle and end which is appropriate for Kindergarten emergent creative writing along the component of Plot. Juxtapose the Kindergartner with the 8th grader who writes a story that involves multiple characters with conflicting and underlying motivations—very sophisticated along the component of Character. The Kindergartners "Bad Guy" versus the 8th graders sophisticated and complex characters reveal that the WWYR contains many levels of narrative writing along the five analytic components providing the teacher with the ability to address, with high specificity, the educational objectives of narrative writing within analytic component. This enables the teacher to developmentally work with students from emergent to advanced and measure growth.

Research Addressing Developmental Validity-

Mott, M.S., Etsler, C., and Drumgold, D. (2003). Applying an analytic writing rubric to children's hypermedia narratives. *Early Childhood Research & Practice*, (5)1. (Online).

Figure 0.16

Concurrent Validity

Definition-

Concurrent validity is the degree to which scores or ratings from one measure align with the results of a comparative measure.

Example Assessment Scenario-

The GRE test for graduate education program admissions has concurrent validity with the XYZ test for education knowledge. Low, medium and high scores on the GRE are highly correlated with low, medium and high scores on hte XYZ.

Test 1 "GRE"	Test 2 "XYZ"

Low, Medium & High Scores for Individuals = Low, Medium & High Scores for the Same

Research Addressing Concurrent Validity-

Mott, M.S., Etsler, C., & Drumgold, D. (2003). Applying an analytic writing rubric to children's hypermedia narratives. *Early Childhood Research & Practice*, (5)1. (Online).

Figure 0.17

Reliability

Definition-

Reliability addresses the repeated consistency or degree to which a measure yields results across similar item types and versions. For example, Student A takes Assessment alternate form/versions X, Y and Z and consistently achieves a similar score. Also, Student A consistently scores at a certain narrow range within version X, Y and Z indicating internal consistency. Reliability, in a nut shell, means that an assessment yields similar results each time it is administered across item type and multiple sections. Thus, for a reliable measure we expect to see similar scores that do not fluctuate more than what typical cognitive growth might yield. See Table 1. Reliability Types below.

Table1

Means and Standard Deviations of Student Essay Performance for Each Topic by Subscale

	GCQ	PK	PN	TX	MI	A	PK test
Civil War (CW)							
Mean[a]	2.48	1.69	1.83	3.11	2.11	2.50	28.32
SD	.72	.78	.57	.97	.89	.70	10.62
Chinese Immigration (CI)							
Mean[a]	2.36	1.24	1.72	3.70	1.57	2.22	15.29
SD	.72	.36	.48	.84	.57	.66	7.96
General Immigration (GI)							
Mean[a]	2.31	1.14	1.77	3.23	1.57	2.24	18.82
SD	.68	.48	.47	1.10	.57	.62	.8.32

Note. Means and standard deviations are averaged across four raters. GCQ = General Content Quality; PK = Prior Knowledge; PN = Number of Principles; TX = Proportion of Text Detail; MI = Misconceptions; A = Argumentation; PK test = Prior Knowledge Test.

a. 5 possible points (Abedi and Baker 1995).

Example Assessment Scenario-

Test-Retest	The same test is administered twice over a period of time to a group and the scores remain stable (positively correlated) over time.
Parallel Forms	Different versions of an assessment are administered and the scores are positively correlated.
Inter-Rater	Different raters/judgments have positively correlated and agreed upon decisions

Reliability is an important technical quality of an assessment that means that results are consistent for individuals and groups within the assessment and across alternate forms and versions. However, reliability does not mean a measure is valid for its intended purpose-it only means that the measure is consistent. Of course, it can be consistently invalid! Thus, we need reliability but to determine what assessment results mean we have to understand validity

[handwritten annotation:] does not mean it is valid for its intended purposes

Reliability ≠ Validity

In order for an assessment to be valid it must indeed be reliable but reliability alone does not constitute validity. For example a telescope that skews 5° to the left consistently yields incorrect measurements of a stars location in the galaxy.

[handwritten annotation:] reliability can yield incorrect measurements consistently

Research Addressing Reliability-

Abedi, J., and Baker, E. L. (1995). A latent-variable modeling approach to assessing interrater reliability, topic generalizability, and validity of a content assessment scoring rubric. *Educational and Psychological Measurement*, 55, 701–715.

Figure 0.18

Value

Definition-

The value of an educational assessment depends on the educational goals underlying the process or moment of assessment and how an assessment is used by various educational constituents: students (increase meta-cognition of what "I" need to learn next?); teachers (what do I need to teach based upon formative results); administrators (are our current educational programs and curriculum effective for the student body and sub-groups of students?); government and agency professionals (are we spending resources on programming and materials wisely?).

Value Sample Scenarios-

Value for?	Sample Scenario
Student	A **formative** assessment on oral reading fluency provides information for the student on how to more effectively read with expression, a key index of fluency.
Teacher	A **developmental** assessment reveals individual student word recognition levels **formatively** throughout the year enabling differentiation of instruction along word attack/recognition. The assessment is **dynamic** in that it requires performance by the student and immediate focused instruction by the classroom teacher.
Administrator	Does the **static** (single snap shot),**summative** and **norm referenced** state-level test reveal an increase in all 3rd grade reading achievement and if not, have we spent our funds wisely on XYZ reading materials?
Community	Do assessment results from**norm reference** and **large-scale** measures reveal needs for transforming schools for educational improvement? Does our educational programming meet the needs of the community for workforce development?
Government	Can we compare **norm referenced** scores or performance of our children with other groups regionally and internationally?

Value for which constituent/s?

Research Addressing Value-

Gearhart, M., Herman, J. L., Novak, J. R., and Wolf, S. A. (1995). Toward the instructional utility of large-scale writing assessment: Validation of a new narrative rubric. *Assessing Writing*, 2, 207–242.

Figure 0.19

Utility

Definition-

The **utility** of an assessment consists of its technical characteristics and specifications based upon validation research. Validation research consists of different things for different assessments. For **norm-referenced** large scale tests the validation process involves reliability and consistency of items within and across similar tests, validation along set criteria and/or statistical analyses of the degree to which content, or a construct, is being measured. Note however that although **summative** or predictive **norm referenced** tests are validated statistically, to ascertain the utility the measurement, **formative** and **performance-based assessments** can receive the same type of rigorous examination.

Measuring Utility-

Reliability	Do items have internal consistency item-to-item and section-to-section? Are results consistent within and between test-takers of similar and different ability or construct under measurement?
Validity	Are results valid similar to other assessments in the same domain (concurrent validity with a similar test?).
Population/Sampling	Do assessment results discriminate ability, sub-groups, language and cultural diversity, content (cognitive/behavioral) or a construct (phonological processing)?

Utility = **Technical Characteristics of the Assessment**

Research Addressing Reliability-

Mott, M.S., Etsler, C., and Drumgold, D. (2003). Applying an analytic writing rubric to children's hypermedia narratives. *Early Childhood Research & Practice*, (5)1. (Online).

Gearhart, M., Herman, J. L., Novak, J. R., and Wolf, S. A. (1995). Toward the instructional utility of large-scale writing assessment: Validation of a new narrative rubric. *Assessing Writing*, 2, 207–242.

Figure 0.20

REFERENCES

Blair, J. and Archer, J. (2001). NEA members denounce high-stakes testing. Available: http://www.edweek.org/ew/ewstory.cfm?slug=42n eatest_web.h20&keywords=National%20Education% 20Association

Brown, L. I., L. Bristol, J. De Four-Babb, J., and D. A. Conrad. "National Tests and Diagnostic Feedback: What Say teachers in Trinidad and Tobago?" *The Journal of Educational Research* 107 (2014): 241–251.

Carmines, Edward G., and Richard A. Zeller (1979). *Reliability and Validity Assessment*. Newbury Park, CA: Sage Publications.

Choppin, J. "Data Use in Practice: Examples from the School Level." Paper presented at the Annual Meeting of the American Educational Research Association, New Orleans, Louisiana, April 2005.

Dunn, K. E., D.T. Airola, W.J. Lo, and M. Garrison. "Becoming Data Driven: The Influence of Teachers' Sense of Efficacy on Concerns Related to Data-Driven Decision Making." *Journal of Experimental Education* 81, no. 2 (2013): 222–241.

Johnson, Peggy E. and Janet H. Chrispeels. "Linking the Central Office and Its Schools for Reform." *Educational Administration Quarterly* 46, no. 5 (2010): 738–775.

Love, Nancy B., Katherine E. Stiles, Susan E. Mundry, and Kathryn DiRanna, eds. *A Data Coach's Guide to Improving Learning for All Students: Unleashing the Power of Collaborative Inquiry*. Thousand Oaks, CA: Corwin, 2008.

Luo, M. "Structural Equation Modeling for High School Principals' Data-Driven Decision Making: An Analysis of Information Use Environments." *Educational Administration Quarterly* 44, no. 5 (2008): 603–634.

Mandinach, Ellen B. "A Perfect Time for Data Use: Using Data-Driven Decision Making to Inform Practice." *Educational Psychologist* 47, no. 2 (2012): 71–85.

Marsh, Julie A., John F. Pane, and Laura S. Hamilton. *Making Sense of Data-Driven Decision Making in Education*. Santa Monica, CA: RAND Corporation, 2006.

Marzano, J. *The Art and Science of Teaching: A Comprehensive Framework for Effective Instruction*. Alexandria, VA: Association for Supervision and Curriculum Development, 2007.

Messick, S. (1989b). Validity. In R. L. Linn (Ed.), *Educational measurement* (3rd ed., pp. 13-103). New York: Macmillan.

Murray, J. "Critical Issues Facing School Leaders Concerning Data-Informed Decision Making." *Professional Educator* 38, no. 1 (2014): 14–22.

National Governors Association Center for Best Practices, Council of Chief State Officers. Common Core State Standards(CCRA:R9): National Governors Association Center for Best Practices, Council of Chief State School Officers, Washington DC. , 2010.

Schifter, C. C., Natarajan, U., Ketelhut, D. J., & Kirchgessner, A. (2014). Data-Driven Decision Making: Facilitating Teacher Use of Student Data to Inform Classroom Instruction. Contemporary Issues in Technology and Teacher Education, 14(4), 419-432.

Stecher, Brian M., and Laura S. Hamilton. Using Test-Score Data in the Classroom (WR-3750EDU). Santa Monica, CA: RAND Education, 2006.

CREDITS

ASSESSMENT EXAMPLE 1. ASSESSMENT OF PHONOLOGICAL AND MORPHOLOGICAL AWARENESS

FROM EARLY LITERACY ASSESSMENT AND TOOLBOX[1]

ELA BACKGROUND

ELA contains two parts, Sound Assessment and Word Parts Assessment, with subskill sections for each part. The assessment is easily administered by a teacher, assistant teacher, or adult volunteer and merely requires that you read the directions, review the practice item with the student, and then proceed to read the one-line questions (or items) to the student, who in turn responds. The student answers questions you read line

Figure 1.1

Assessmet Toolbox Book (small)

for line to the best of their ability, and you record correct/incorrect, using the answer in bold embedded for you in each section of the assessment.

Throughout the school year, it is recommended that you assess your students intermittently (every other month) to determine which reading skills you should focus on for their instruction, and this process should be used to complement your comprehensive reading program already in place. Other reading areas of phonics, fluency, vocabulary, and comprehension are positively impacted by assessing and teaching Sound Assessment and Word Parts Assessment. Differentiation in reading instruction is not always easy to accomplish, and using the ELA results to point you to the exact corresponding learning module/reading game (or "minilesson") will support you in teaching directly in the area of student reading-skill need.

The following section is extracted from the SAGE Open article "Technical Examination of a Measure of Phonological Sensitivity" by Michael S. Mott and Angela S. Rutherford.

ELA RESEARCH[2] FOR ASSESSMENT OF PHONOLOGICAL SKILL

Little doubt exists that phonological processing ability is a prerequisite for early reading success. With the publication of the influential National Reading Panel Report in 2000 synthesizing research from the 1990s, attention rightfully focused on the most complex phonological skill, phonemic awareness (PM) and the corresponding positive correlations to phonics (Ball and Blachman 1991; Bentin and Leshem 1993; Blachman, Ball, Black, and Tangel 1994; Griffith 1991; Torgesen, Morgan, and Davis 1992; Treiman and Baron 1983). However, research is now pointing educators to the premise that phonological sensitivity (PS) is holistically important to early literacy success in English (Anthony, Williams, McDonald, and Francis 2007), Spanish (Anthony et al. 2006), and Greek (Aidinis and Nunes 2001). The phrase *phonological sensitivity* better illustrates the phonological processing abilities related to how children develop, mentally navigate, and work with sound units. Stanovich's (1992) earlier and Pufpaff's (2009) recent advocacy of PS as a term to describe the two different components typical of phonological processing offer a dual conception for PS. The two latent variables that make up a single unidimensional PS construct are *phonological awareness* (PG) and *phonemic awareness*. Applied research (Bryant, MacLean, Bradley, and Crossland 1990; Burgess and Lonigan 1998; Lonigan, Burgess, and Anthony 2000) and meta-analyses (Burgess 2006; National Early Literacy Panel 2008; Pufpaff 2009) provide evidence that PS develops along a progression and that success at the beginning levels of PS predicts success at the more advanced levels. Indeed, Carroll, Snowling, Hulme, and Stevenson (2003) and others (Blachman 2000; Bryant et al. 1990; Byrne and Fielding-Barnsley 1991, 1993) found that achievement in PG led to achievement in PM. In addition, PS acquired in a bidirectional manner (Burgess and Lonigan 1998) generally following a developmental pattern of "shallow" or rudimentary word-unit sounds (do these two words rhyme?) to "deep" individual sounds (what sound do you hear at the end of h-a-t?) Anthony et al. 2002. Webb, Schwanenflugel, and Kim (2004) similarly discerned the correlation between phonological skill and later phonemic skill and their corresponding predictive relationship to alphabetic knowledge.

The National Early Literacy Panel (2008) concluded that PG (rhyme, syllables, onset-rime, phonemes) has a significant relationship to decoding and reading comprehension (with rhyme being the weakest link to decoding skills). As mentioned earlier, the National Reading Panel (2000) also concluded that PM (phoneme isolation, manipulation, and segmentation) was a predictor of early reading success as measured via children's competency in decoding phonics. When children understand phonemes, their ability to understand phonics is greatly enhanced. In fact, Juel (1988) stated, "without phonemic awareness, phonics instruction is meaningless" (p. 410). Furthermore, the National Reading Panel (2000) clearly delineated the robust relationship between phonics and learning to read. It is with this developmental progression from a general or shallow PS to a more refined or deeper sense of phonemes to the more sophisticated ability to understand phonics (sound *and* symbol relationships) that children learn to negotiate the difficult task of decoding words. While PS at the PG level is not directly linked to the phonics skills learned to decode words, PG is directly linked to PM skills that in turn are linked to phonics skills (Carroll et al. 2003). With this insight, researchers and educators are now advocating assessment and instruction in the full PS continuum to leverage the phonological ability of children to promote later, more advanced knowledge of PM, which leads to achievement in phonics. Once children become proficient and automatic word decoders, they become more able to focus on the task of reading comprehension—the ultimate goal of reading.

The plethora of phonological screens (Yopp 1995), tests (Watkins and Edwards 2004), and assessments (Torgesen and Bryant 2004) developed by psychologists, psychometricians, educational psychologists, and communication disorders professionals tend to focus on the identification of PA *deficits* and corresponding need for intervention. Recently, researchers have identified the need to apply a developmental conceptualization of PS that dictates the need for tools to teach (and measure) PS (Anthony, Lonigan, Driscoll, Phillips, and Burgess 2003; Cassady, Smith, and Putman 2008). In this vein, the Leveled Assessment of Phonological Sensitivity (ELA) was designed to assess the continuum of PS as advocated by Torgesen et al. (1992) and Pufpaff (2009).

PS AS A DEVELOPMENTAL PROGRESSION

Pufpaff (2009) suggested that "insufficient attention is being paid to the developmental nature of phonological sensitivity skills" (p. 679). Researchers (Anthony et al. 2002, 2003; Byrnes and Wasik 2009; Carroll et al. 2003; Lonigan et al. 2000) have discussed the developmental nature of PS as a progression that begins with a child's ability to analyze larger units of sound and progressively continues in difficulty until a child can analyze the smallest units of sound (phonemes). Byrnes and Wasik (2009) stated that "between the ages of one and seven, children seem to progress from the ability to recognize whole words to the ability to recognize progressively smaller portions of words (e.g., whole words to syllables, onsets and rimes, to eventually phonemes)" (p. 58). Generally, children are able to work with larger phonological units before smaller phonological units.

Currently, a developmental focus on PS is being advocated to better prepare children to develop the more difficult tasks involved in manipulating individual sounds or phonemes (Anthony et al. 2003; Carroll, Snowling, and Hulme 2003; Cassady et al. 2008; Pufpaff 2009). This focus stems from the research supporting PS as a unidimensional construct that develops along a continuum from less to more complex tasks. Once educators understand this continuum, they are more likely to assess children's PS and use the assessment data to plan explicit instruction focusing on children's developmental needs. In fact, the authors of the National Early Literacy Panel's (2008) report stated that "what is more likely more important is that the assessment and instructional activities occur within a child's development level along the developmental continuum" (p. 77). PS instruction is beneficial for most, if not all, children and is absolutely necessary for others who are at risk for experiencing reading difficulties. Without this very foundational knowledge of the sound structure of language, children will likely experience reading difficulties. Since PS develops along a continuum, assessment devices should address all the levels within the construct of PS as described by researchers. These tools should be available to use for screening and progress monitoring along that developmental continuum; thus, the assessment needs multiple forms that discriminate among the different developmental levels so that individual student needs can be addressed via explicit and systematic instruction that is fun and engaging for students.

TRANSLATING RESEARCH INTO PRACTICE
OVERVIEW

For research to affect educator practice, reading researchers and experts are called on to make research available to educators in ways that help them understand how the research should look in classroom practice. In the case of PS, it is imperative that educators understand the dynamics of PS related to the progression of skills. This is no easy task, as Phillips, Clancy-Menchetti, and Lonigan (2008) related:

> One pragmatic implication of this continuum of phonological awareness along levels of linguistic complexity and cognitive operation is that at any given point in time, a classroom of preschool children will include children at numerous points along the continuum (p. 2).

In addition, researchers must be able to adequately explain PS so that educators understand PS and are not confused by the plethora of terms used to describe PS. If PS is thoroughly understood, educators will be better able to recognize the different levels of PS and apply that knowledge in their classroom instruction and assessment. With a comprehensive understanding of PS, educational professionals can apply the research so they know what they are teaching, what they are measuring, why they are teaching it, and why they are measuring it in ways that effectively meet students' instructional needs.

It is important that educators understand the development continuum through which young children proceed in acquiring phonological skills. This understanding will result in the use of assessment tools and techniques for documenting children's PS progress and for identifying those children who are not progressing to the appropriate developmental level. By identifying those children who have problems and pinpointing the PS level at which those problems exist, educators can plan appropriate, focused instruction to support the PS development necessary for early reading success.

Despite the significant body of evidence supporting the notion that PS skills should be taught and assessed, many early childhood educators lack the competencies to differentiate developmental PS instruction (Dickinson and Brady 2005; Moats and Foorman 2003; Zill and Resnick 2006). Due to educators' lack of understanding, a formative classroom PS assessment can anchor and focus educators within a usable framework; this echoes Ganske's (1993) call for a developmental spelling assessment to assist educators in making sense of the developmental progression of children's orthographic knowledge. One could argue that prior to Ganske's (2000) articulation and system (*Word Journeys*) for enabling teachers to *easily* level the developmental spelling ability of all classroom students, a teacher would have to be exceedingly clever to know the level of orthographic knowledge of each student based on a comparison of developmental writing stage descriptions from research and the actual students' writing samples in the classroom.

FORMATIVE ASSESSMENT

The idea of connecting a formative assessment "teaching tool" to technical characteristics usually reserved for norm-referenced measures is not new. To make research more practical for educators, researchers have attempted to bridge the divide between assessment designed to inform policy and assessment designed to improve educational practice so that formative assessments could serve the dual purpose of guiding learning and informing policy decisions for educational reform. In this vein, rigorous and convincing reliability and validity characteristics exist for collections of children's narratives (Gearhart, Herman, Novak, and Wolf 1995; Novak, Herman, and Gearhart 1996), collections of narrative writing with media elements (Mott, Etsler, and Drumgold 2003), developmental spelling (Ganske 1999), and, more recently, with districtwide performance-based assessment connecting high-quality assessment for large-scale policy decision making (Niemi, Baker, and Sylvester 2007). The above examples represent a mere sampling of assessments developed as part of, or influenced by, research from the Center for Research on Evaluations, Standards, and Student Testing (CRESST) that advocates appropriate assessment use and development for improving teaching and learning.

ASSESSMENT FOR GUIDING INSTRUCTION

To effectively plan instruction that pinpoints the appropriate PS level for children's developmental progression, formative assessment or performance-based assessment tools are effective because they link teacher–student language to educational objectives. Formative assessments are not used to assign grades but are used to determine the child's skill level for targeted, differentiated instruction. Once the assessment data is collected, educators can use the data to ascertain whether the child needs additional instruction on that particular skill or needs to move forward to more challenging levels of skill attainment. Thus, formative assessment tools and techniques assist educators in planning future instruction to match children's developmental needs.

Salinger (2006) stated that classroom-based assessments should "accommodate the dynamic nature of young learners' progression from preliteracy to literacy. The tests would be quick and easy to administer, score, and interpret; and data would have immediate utility to teachers" (p. 430). Also according to Salinger (2006), for teachers to use the data immediately, they would need to be trained to "give the tests and understand the results" (p. 430). Although classroom-based assessments may not typically contain the full gamut of psychometric properties, these assessments usually possess "*face* validity." However, for the current assessment, the researchers seek to establish more rigorous validity characteristics along the hierarchy of validity, with the corresponding psychometric data as the basis for promoting its use.

INSTRUCTIONAL SENSITIVITY OF AN INSTRUMENT

According to Niemi, Wang, Steinberg, Baker, and Wang (2007), validation of an instrument is dependent on the degree to which it supports teacher "instructional sensitivity" along a construct domain in a given curriculum. The current instrument has been designed to address, in a fine-toothed manner, the continuum of PS addressed above. Accordingly, "when assessments … are intended to guide and improve instruction, the sensitivity of the assessment(s) to instruction is an essential piece of the evidence needed to validate them" (Niemi et al. 2007, p. 216). Niemi et al. argue that if schools are expected to improve along educational outcomes, the assessment tool must be aligned to the instructional objective. Believing that alignment is critical, the current assessment tool includes classroom teacher feedback as well as validity analyses. In addition, participant-teachers (*n* = 28) assisted in capturing the instructional sensitivity of the ELA via their classroom use following the Niemi et al. "opportunity to learn" (OTL) study format enabling teachers to capture experiences of students encountering the assessment under investigation (p. 216).

CONTENT KNOWLEDGE RELATED TO PS

Pufpaff (2009) conducted a literature review that incorporates the last thirty years of research related to PS in an effort to translate the research base for educators into the knowledge they need to effectively address the phonological developmental needs of students in their classrooms. PS is defined as "encompassing both phonological and phonemic awareness" (Pufpaff 2009, p. 679). Both of these terms refer to an individual's ability to work with the sounds of the English language without print involvement. Within the research literature, the terms *phonological awareness* and *phonemic awareness* have been used incorrectly and often interchangeably. As a result, educators who seek to understand phonological development are often confused about the instruction and assessment techniques that are appropriate for their students. Due to the confusion related to the use of the terms, the

International Reading Association (1998) issued a position statement that defined PG as encompassing "larger units of sound as well, such as syllables, onsets, and rimes" (p. 3). The International Reading Association also stated that "phonemic awareness refers to an understanding about the smallest units of sound that make up the speech stream: phonemes" (p. 3). More recent research (Anthony et al. 2003; Anthony et al. 2007; Byrnes and Wasik 2009; Carroll et al. 2003; Lonigan, Burgess, and Anthony 2000) has pointed reading researchers to the notion that PS actually exists along a developmental continuum that begins with PG (units of sound larger than individual phonemes) and progressively emerges to the more complex PM (individual phonemes). In translating this research into classroom practice, educators must understand this increasingly complex developmental progression of PS to better develop instructional and assessment practices to meet the needs of young learners sitting in classrooms.

PS CONTINUUM INFLUENCES ON ASSESSMENT, INSTRUCTION, AND INTERVENTION

Armed with a clearer understanding of the PS developmental continuum, appropriate assessment, instruction, and intervention practices can be developed and implemented. Before instruction can occur, educators must use assessment data to better serve students' needs. Assessment tools should address all levels of the PS continuum for maximum benefit to teachers and students. Table 1.1 illustrates this synthesis: (a) ELA item types capturing the full PS continuum in hierarchical order, (b) the relationship of ELA item types to the body of research and PS assessments since 1976 as comprehensively addressed by Pufpaff (2009), and (c) the development and rationale of ELA levels and rationalized differences with Pufpaff's summary in consideration of the body of research.

ELA: MOVING CHILDREN FROM LOWER-LEVEL TO HIGHER-LEVEL PS SKILL

PS AS A CONTINUUM: DEVELOPING INVENTORY LEVELS

In developing the ELA (see Figure 1.1), Pufpaff's (2009) synthesis of the research base provided insight into the different PS levels and the linguistic and cognitive complexity within the levels. A comparison of the PS levels assessed on ELA and levels as defined by Pufpaff (2009) is described in Table 1.1. As documented in Table 1.1., ELA follows Pufpaff's articulation of PS developmental levels, except that ELA collapses several of Pufpaff's levels into one level for the purpose of making the tool more accessible for teachers during classroom assessment and instruction. For example, Pufpaff describes five levels of rhyming skills (rhyme detection to rhyme oddity), but the ELA includes the one rhyming skill level (rhyme detection) that progressively becomes more difficult within the rhyme detection skill level. Another difference in ELA and Pufpaff's progression is that the ELA includes alliteration. Many researchers (Bryant et al. 1990; Chard and Dickson 1999; Moats and Tolman 2009) include alliteration in the development continuum. In addition, ELA uses developmental progression of rhyme, words in a sentence, syllables, and onset-rime, whereas Pufpaff describes the progression from rhyme, syllable blending, words in a sentence, and syllables. However, others (Byrnes and Wasik 2009; Moats and Tolman 2009) explain the development progression that compares with the levels in the ELA—words in a sentence, syllables, and onset-rime progression. Key studies informing the structure of the ELA within item-type characteristics were Chafouleas, VanAuken, and Dunham's (2001) and Cassady et al.'s (2008) examinations of the effects of linguistic complexity, manipulation type, and the corresponding influence on difficulty. ELA within items along each type or "level" move from easier to more difficult based on the findings by Chafouleas et al. and Cassady et al., which suggested the easy-to-difficult structure of blending, segmenting, and deletion by initial, final, or medial sound.

RHYMING WITH SIMPLE WORDS! - 1-			
date	student	teacher	
Skill Focus: RHYME			Correct = √
Practice: *"The two words that I am going to say may or may not rhyme, so listen carefully. Do lot and pot rhyme!" - (pause)- "Yes"*			
-1- Do pat and mat rhyme? (Yes)			

Figure 1.2

Table 1.1. Comparison of the Developmental Sequence of Phonological Sensitivity Skills

LAPS ITEM-TYPE SKILL	PUFPAFF (2009) SKILL*	LAPS EXAMPLES
Phonological PgA rhyme	Rhyme detection Rhyme creation Rhyme production Rhyme recognition	Do hat and cat rhyme? (yes)
PgB alliteration	Not included; however, research by Adams (1990) Bryant. MacLean. Bradley, and Crossland (1990) and Moats and Tolman (2009) support alliteration	Do all three words start with the same sound? bat. ball, small? (yes)
PgC words PgD syllables	Sentence segmentation Compound word Multisyllabic	If you take "pig" out of "piglet" what do you have? (let)
PgE onsets and rimes	Syllable blending	What word do these sounds put together make: b-it? (bit)
Phonemic PmA isolation	Phoneme isolation but Pufpaff (2009) has this task placed fourth in her developmental progression. However. Vandervelden and Siegel (1995) provide evidence that phoneme recognition (the LAPS's phoneme isolation task) as the least complex in the phonemic awareness tasks	What sound do you hear at the beginning of bear. bun. bin? (/b/)
PmB identification	Sound to word matching	What is the same sound in the following words: ban; bit; bun? (/b/)
PmC categorization	Word to word matching	Which word does not belong: can. cat bug? (bug)
PmD blending	Phoneme blending but Pufpaff (2009) has this task placed first in her developmental progression. However, the LAPS places blending following isolation, identification, and categorization because blending is a more complex phonemic awareness task as described by Chard and Dickson (1999) and Cassady. Smith, and Huber (2005)	What word can you make from the following sounds:/b/./a/./t/? (bat)
PmE segmenting	Phoneme counting	How many sounds do you hear in "pen"? (3)
PmF manipulation	Phoneme deletion	Say the word "bat" without the /b/. (at)
	Phoneme Substitution Phoneme reversal—The LAPS does not include this task	Say the word "fist" without the /s/. (fit)

Note: LAPS = Leveled Assessment of Phonological Sensitivity: PS = phonological sensitivity.
*Table 1.1 synthesizes the LAPS PS continuum by skill type with Pufpaff's (2009) comprehensive compilation of PS skill levels integrating the body of PS research addressing the nature of the continuum (Fox and Routh 1976; Goldstein 1976; Helfgott 1976; Lewkowicz and Low l979; Liberman, Shankweiler, Fischer, and Carter 1974; Rosner and Simon 1971; Seymour and Evans 1994; Skjelfjord 1976; Stahl and Murray 1994; Stanovich, Cunningham and Cramer 1984; Vandervelden and Siegel 1995; and Yopp 1988).

the items are related to one another, a key indicator of reliability. Less variance across items provides insight into the reliability of the ELA.

Cronbach's alpha and Guttman's split-half coefficients were high (α = .93 and .95), indicating convincing evidence for ELA internal consistency across all completed forms (n = 122). ELA internal consistency is higher than the level of Watkins and Edwards's (2004) alpha coefficient of .89 for the Mountain Shadows Phonemic Awareness Scale (MS-PAS). In addition, ELA measures are higher than the Test of Phonological Awareness Second Edition Plus (Torgesen and Bryant 2004), which has an alpha coefficient of .8. validity of the ELA: Torgesen, Wagner, Rashotte, Burgess, and Hecht's (1997) and Pufpaff's (2009) definition and articulation of PS skills, and Pufpaff's meta-analysis of the body of PS item types studied over four decades. Table 1.1 provides the context for ELA item type and rationale for how item types are leveled by difficulty along the PS continuum.

DEVELOPMENTAL VALIDITY

Given the assumption that older (Grade 2) children have more highly developed phonology than younger children (Pre-K), one might expect to see a significant difference between ELA scores along grade levels Pre-K–2. Although chronological age does not always positively correlate with cognition, the general phonological developmental milestones have been established in numerous studies (Yopp 1988, and most notably in Burgess and Lonigan 1998). Two ANOVA tests were conducted to determine the developmental sensitivity of ELA scores to the grade level of participants for (a) phonological "Pg" and (b) phonemic "Pm" item types. A significant difference between grade levels along Pg (A–E) and Pm (A–F) item types (see Table 1.1 and Figure 1.2 for identifying Pg and Pm type for P-label) would indicate developmental sensitivity of the ELA.

The analyses were significant for all five Pg item types: PgA $F(3, 324)$ = 8.23, p = .001; PgB $F(3, 324)$ = 2.62, p = .05; PgC $F(3, 324)$ = 4.99, p = .02; PgD $F(3, 322)$ = 7.22, p = .001; and PgE $F(3, 323)$ = 7.70, p = .001. Tukey HSD tests were used to follow up these effects and were significant between Pre-K and all grade levels for PgA, PgC, and PgE but not PgB and PgD. For example, for "PgA" items, Pre-K children scored lower than K (d = −2.08, SE = .62, p = .05); Grade 1 (d = −1.75, SE = .60, p = .02); and Grade 2 (d = −2.78, SE = .59, p = .001). In addition, Grade 1 children scored lower on PgA than Grade 2 children (d = −1.03, SE = .35, p = .02), but children in K did not score lower than Grade 1 children (d = .33, SE = .39, p = .82). The statistically significant mean differences (d) indicate that younger children scored lower than older children, providing evidence for the developmental sensitivity of ELA Pg items between Pre-K and Grade 2 and all other grades, Pre-K and K, Grades 1 and 2, but not K and 1. It is important to note, however, that mean scores across all grade levels Pre-K to 1 for all ELA items were higher for each grade level. For Grades 1 to 2, mean scores reached a plateau, indicating that ELA Pg items do not have developmental sensitivity above Grade 1.

The lack of discrimination between PgB (alliteration) and PgD (syllables) supports research indicating that (PgB) alliteration is closely related to rhyme and more difficult to discriminate (Bryant et al. 1990). The lack of discrimination between K and 1 could be explained by the time of year that the pilot study was conducted. Since K students would have more experience with PS by the middle of the second semester, those discriminatory factors could have dissipated due to progression along the continuum.

Similar to the Pg item types, analyses were significant for all six Pm item types: PmA $F(3, 324) = 6.70$, $p = .001$; PmB $F(3, 323) = 6.08$, $p = .001$; PmC $F(3, 324) = 7.39$, $p = .001$; PmD $F(3, 324) = 9.37$, $p = .001$; PmE $F(3, 321) = 7.19$, $p = .001$; and PmF $F(3, 324) = 9.55$, $p = .001$. Tukey HSD tests were used to follow up these effects and were significant between Pre-K across all grade levels and between K and 1 for PmC ($d = -1.90$, $SE = .72$, $p = .04$) and PmD ($d = -3.56$, $SE = .83$ $p = .01$). For example, for "PmA" items, Pre-K children scored lower than K ($d = -4.09$, $SE = 1.2$, $p = .05$), Grade 1 ($d = -5.2$, $SE = 1.2$, $p = .001$), and Grade 2 ($d = -4.09$, $SE = 1.2$, $p = .05$). The statistically significant mean differences (d) between Pre-K and Grades K–2 provide evidence that younger children scored lower than older children (thus the negative values in d), indicating the developmental sensitivity of ELA Pm items between grades Pre-K and all other grades. It must be noted, however, that for "Pm" phonemic item types, with inherently more difficult linguistic complexity and cognitive operation levels, that Pre-K and K respondents received lower scores than Grade 1 and 2 students without significant results, possibly due to the "discontinue rule" (see Webb et al. 2004), which effectively stopped assessment, leaving Pre-K and K student response rates very low for Pm levels.

The above results support other research that global PS develops along a continuum, with the global Pg developing prior to the more sophisticated Pm (Anthony et al. 2003, 2007; Byrnes and Wasik 2009; Carroll et al. 2003; Lonigan et al. 2000). Due to the discontinue rule, students in Pre-K and K did not continue with the assessment, which certainly follows previous research findings that few preschool and kindergarten children are able to work at the phoneme level (Pufpaff 2009).

DISCRIMINANT VALIDITY

Convergent validity—the degree to which operations of a measure are related to operations from another measure, or even within a measure—determines the relatedness or degree that items *converge*, indicating that what is being measured across the instrument is indeed one construct. The notion that the ELA measures a unidimensional construct domain of PS would support previous research (most notably, Torgesen and Burgess 1992 and Pufpaff 2009). Discriminant validity—the degree to which items on a test possess sensitivity to specific areas or subdomains (ELA item types PgA to PmF) intended by the test designers—would indicate, for example, the sensitivity of the instrument to discriminate between PG and PM. In addition, discriminant validity would provide evidence that ELA item types are assessing subtypes within the continuum of PS. Both divergent and discriminant validity provide support for the construct validity of ELA. Construct validity is the degree to which an assessment measures the construct (PS) that it is designed to measure.

Confirmatory factor analysis (CFA) with structural equation modeling (SEM) was utilized to determine the ability of three predefined factor models to fit an observed set of data. Specifically, how do ELA levels (factor indicators) relate to latent factors of PS identified in the literature? CFA enables researchers to assess multiple models to address discriminant and convergent validity for a single- or multiple-factor model. The ability to test the significance of specific factor-loading combinations (such as phonological and phonemic double factors; phonological, phonemic, and onset-rime triple factors; or PS as a single factor) leads to the ability to frame the convergent and discriminant validity of the instrument. CFA was selected versus exploratory factor analyses due to the significant volume of research in PA addressing the developmental continuum and test, screen, and assessment item characteristics since 1976. Armed with this well-established theoretical base, three CFA models were hypothesized to incrementally scrutinize ELA factor indicators (item types/levels) to the theorized psychological construct of PA. The researchers, adhering to the cautionary advice of Thompson and Borello (1989), designed more than one model to avoid assumptions that only a single model fits the data.

The theoretical basis for ELA item categories and item characteristics addressing the PS continuum incrementally from research point to content validity in general from the genesis of the ELA discussed earlier. To further explore validity, exploratory factor analysis was conducted to determine simple patterns and patterns of relationships among ELA levels. Can ELA levels (variables) be explained largely in terms of a much smaller number of factors (variables)? Thus, this factor analysis seeks to heuristically unearth patterns and relationships from many dependent variables (ELA levels) to discern something about the nature of the independent latent (factors) that affect them. Unlike multidimensional scaling, in factor analysis, two variables cannot be organized along one cluster, thus enabling insight into each variable's tendency to load with a factor.

Results of the CFA factor loadings revealed a one-factor solution, indicating that PS consists of a unidimensional construct domain, although rhyme received the lowest correlation (see descriptive statistics in Table 1.2 for means, standard deviations across ELA types). SEM was utilized to visually portray CFA results along pathways as correlational coefficients. The goal is to visually portray and evaluate the latent variable in light of the factors. Thus, the bubble represents PS latent variables in Model 1, the two bubbles represent Phonological and Phonemic latent variables in Model 2, and the three bubbles represent Phonological, Onset-Rime, and Phonemic latent variables in Model 3. The square shapes represent the dependent variables, which are the eleven item types consisting of phonological and phonemic categories (PgA through PmF; see Tables 1.3 and 1.4).

SEM was utilized to visually portray CFA results along pathways as correlational coefficients. Three models of PS were tested: (a) PS as a unidimensional construct, (b) PG and PM as two separate constructs, and (3) PG, Onset-Rime, and PM as a construct. The structural equation model results (see Table 1.5) reveal qualities of "fit" or the extent to which the proposed

Table 1.2. LAPS Descriptive Statistics for Phonological and Phonemic Items

PHONOLOGICAL AWARENESS ("PG")	n	M	SD	95% CONFIDENCE INTERVAL FOR MEAN	
				LOWER BOUND	UPPER BOUND
PgA					
Pre-K	23	9.78	3.233	8.38	11.18
K	83	11.87	2.305	11.36	12.37
First	101	11.53	2.795	10.98	12.09
Second	121	12.57	2.572	12.11	13.03
Total	328	11.88	2.715	11.58	12.17
PgB					
Pre-K	22	8.4545	4.79809	6.3272	10.5819
K	83	10.8675	3.54336	10.0938	11.6412
First	101	10.1782	3.00798	9.5844	10.7720
Second	121	10.3636	3.90299	9.6611	11.0661
Total	327	10.3058	3.65264	9.9084	10.7032
PgC					
Pre-K	23	4.9565	4.95872	2.8122	7.1008
K	53	8.0964	4.86805	7.0334	9.1594
First	101	9.2574	5.04907	8.2607	10.2542
Second	121	9.0826	5.45678	8.1005	10.0648
Total	328	8.5976	5.24765	8.0275	9.1676
PgD					
Pre-K	23	4.2609	4.96549	2.1136	6.4081
K	82	6.9157	5.40597	5.7352	8.0961
First	101	8.6436	4.90629	7.6750	9.6121
Second	119	9.3782	6.33392	8.2283	10.5280
Total	326	8.1626	5.75350	7.5357	8.7895
PgE					
Pre-K	23	3.0870	4.69926	1.0548	5.1191
K	83	7.2048	6.29122	5.8311	8.5785
First	100	9.2800	5.78238	8.1326	10.4274
Second	121	8.7934	6.26620	7.6655	9.9213
Total	327	8.1376	6.21566	7.4614	8.8138
				95% CONFIDENCE INTERVAL FOR MEAN	

(continued)

PHONEMIC AWARENESS ("PM")	n	M	SD	SE	LOWER BOUND	UPPER BOUND
PmA						
Pre-K	23	2.4348	3.43546	.71634	.9492	3.9204
K	83	6.5301	5.67050	.62242	5.2919	7.7683
First	101	7.6931	4.81610	.47922	6.7423	8.6438
Second	121	7.3967	5.66492	.51499	6.3770	8.4163
Total	328	6.9207	5.42673	.29964	6.3313	7.5102
PmB						
Pre-K	23	2.3043	3.56032	.74238	.7647	3.8439
K	83	5.5060	5.01795	.55079	4.4103	6.6017
First	101	6.5941	4.78368	.47599	5.6497	7.5384
Second	120	7.0833	5.93463	.54176	6.0106	8.1561
Total	327	6.1957	5.34729	.29571	5.6140	6.7775
PmC						
Pre-K	23	1.6522	1.89757	.39567	.8316	2.4727
K	83	3.8193	4.49971	.49391	2.8367	4.8018

				95% CONFIDENCE INTERVAL FOR MEAN	
PHONOLOGICAL AWARENESS ("PG")	n	M	SD	LOWER BOUND	UPPER BOUND
First	101	5.7228	4.72042	.46970	4.7909	6.6546
Second	121	5.9256	5.60382	.50944	4.9170	6.9343
Total	328	5.0305	5.02766	.27761	4.4844	5.5766
PmD						
Pre-K	23	2.0870	3.60445	.75158	.5283	3.6456
K	83	3.5783	4.79614	.52644	2.5310	4.6256
First	101	7.1386	5.82414	.57952	5.9889	8.2884
Second	121	6.1157	6.26656	.56969	4.9878	7.2436
Total	328	5.5061	5.84405	.32268	4.8713	6.1409
PmE						
Pre-K	23	1.8261	2.93338	.61165	.5576	3.0946
K	83	4.0602	5.68556	.62407	2.8188	5.3017
First	98	7.0000	5.70404	.57620	5.8564	8.1436
Second	121	5.7273	6.13596	.55781	4.6228	6.8317
Total	325	5.4092	5.88484	.32643	4.7670	6.0514

PmF						
Pre-K	23	1.4783	1.90381	.39697	.6550	2.3015
K	83	2.6627	3.41545	.37489	1.9169	3.4084
First	101	5.6139	4.93755	.49130	4.6391	6.5856
Second	121	5.1322	5.77198	.52473	4.0933	6.1712
Total	328	4.3994	4.98704	.27536	3.8577	4.9411

Note: LAPS = Leveled Assessment of Phonological Sensitivity.

Table 1.3. LAPS Reliability Analyses

RELIABILITY STATISTICS: INTERNAL CONSISTENCY AND GUNMAN'S SPLIT-HALF RELIABILITY	
Cronbach's alpha	
Part 1	
Value	.931
No. of items	6[a]
Part 2	
Value	.880
No. of items	5[b]
Total no. of items	11
Correlation between forms	
Spearrnan-Brown coefficient	.902
Equal length	.949
Unequal length	.949
Guttman split-half coefficient	.947

Note: LAPS = Leveled Assessment of Phonological Sensitivity.
[a]The items are PgA, PgB, PgC, PgD, PgE, PmA.
[b]The kerns are PmB, PmC, PmD, PmE, PmF.

Table 1.4. Covariance—Variance Matrix of LAPS Item Types

CORRELATION	PgA	PgB	PgC	PgD	PgE	PmA	PmB	PmC	PmD	PmE	PmF
PgA	1.000	.823	.728	.719	.752	.638	.664	.584	.696	.762	.611
PgB	.823	1.000	.686	.682	.670	.662	.663	.587	.627	.712	.539
PgC	.728	.686	1.000	.647	.754	.651	.666	.697	.711	.693	.658
PgD	.719	.682	.647	1.000	.708	.634	.715	.592	.657	.550	.662
PgE	.752	.670	.754	.708	1.000	.712	.694	.585	.800	.718	.597
PmA	.638	.662	.651	.634	.712	1.000	.734	557	.563	.629	.476
PmB	.664	.663	.666	.715	.694	.734	1.000	.596	.666	.654	.629
PmC	.584	.587	.697	.592	.585	.557	.596	1.000	.561	.563	.538
PmD	.696	.627	.711	.657	.800	.563	.666	.561	1.000	.656	.604
PmE	.762	.712	.693	.550	.718	.629	.654	.563	.656	1.000	.575
PmF	.611	.539	.658	.662	.597	.476	.629	.538	.604	.575	1.000

Note: LAPS = Leveled Assessment of Phonological Sensitivity.

Table 1.5. Comparisons of Fit Indices for Models Examining the Distinguishableness of LAPS Levels With PS Domains

MODEL NUMBER AND DESCRIPTION	df	CFI	TU	RMSEA
1. One-factor first-order only model PS, g	45	.88	.83	.08
2. Two-factor model first-order only model PHGL, PHNMC, g	43	.76	.63	.29
3. Three-factor first-order only model PHGL, RIME, PHNMC, g	45	.77	.76	.12

Note: LAPS = Leveled Assessment of Phonological Sensitivity; CFI = comparative fit index; RMSEA = root mean square error of approximation; PS = phonological sensitivity.

RHYMING WITH SIMPLE WORDS! - 1-			
date	student	teacher	
Skill Focus: SYLLABLES			Correct = √
Practice: "Blend together the words that you hear (farm; house to farmhouse), segment (backbone to back; bone), or remove a word airplane without air; plane)."			
-1- Listen to these two words: gem; stone. Say the entire word together (gemstone).			
-2- Listen to these two words: *hair; cut*. Say the entire word together (haircut).			

Figure 1.3

DISCUSSION OF ELA VALUE AND UTILITY

VALUE (HELPFULNESS OF MEASURE)

The value or helpfulness of a measure is determined by whether the measure or assessment tool builds teacher knowledge, pinpoints student knowledge, and affects teacher practice (Novak et al. 1996). Will the tool affect classroom practice? ELA provides a formative, performance-based assessment that links teacher–student language to educational objectives. Just as Ganske's (1999) spelling assessment provides a tool for determining students' developmental spelling level that guides instructional delivery and provides common language for teacher and student, the ELA serves as a tool for determining students' PS level for determining initial instruction as well as continuing instruction. In addition, ELA can be used as a progress-monitoring tool to determine students' progress along the developmental continuum and to affect instructional decisions. Salinger (2006) stated that classroom-based assessments should follow the developmental progression of literacy tasks, the ELA provides that fluid movement of PS development.

UTILITY (TECHNICAL QUALITIES)

The utility of an assessment tool has been defined as a product of its reliability, validity, cost-effectiveness, acceptability, and educational impact (Gearhart et al. 1995). According to Salinger (2006), assessments should be quick and easy to administer, score, and interpret and have immediate utility to teachers. ELA provides evidence of the characteristics defined as important for assessment utility. As described previously in the article, ELA reliability and validity measures are robust. In addition, teachers accepted ELA during the pilot program with positive comments about the tool. Finally, ELA can provide educational impact when teachers utilize the data to inform instructional decisions.

ELA PHONOLOGICAL SECTION RESEARCH CONCLUSIONS

The goal of this study is to bring the research base into the classroom where teachers are able to use ELA as an "in practice" tool, as opposed to sole reliance on tests, screens, and inventories designed to identify *deficits*. ELA was created as a tool to assist teachers in making instructional decisions as well as in communicating with students (in the form of instructional prompts) and colleagues along the PS continuum in ways that mirror a phonics curriculum without the presence of letter symbols. Given students' developmental nature and students' variability with experience to spoken language, teachers must differentiate instruction along a specific learning domain (in this case PS) to scaffold individual students' ability to reach higher levels of sensitivity. For scaffolding to occur, assessment must support teachers' ability to make data-based decisions that focus instruction on the needs of the learner. The ELA can be used in ways that support teachers in their quest to provide PS instruction that is based on individual student data.

model fits the distribution according to the articulated construct. In the case of the current study, the authors proposed three models as suggested in Yaun (2005) and followed Yaun's protocol for qualifying goodness of fit. Goodness of fit can be viewed as how trustworthy a given model is in terms of how well it fits the scores or results in juxtaposition to the corresponding theoretical rationale for those scores. Yaun, in his review of structural equation model results interpretation, found that generally, comparative fit index (CFI) and TFI scores above .90 are acceptable and root mean square error of approximation (RMSEA) scores close to .05 are also acceptable. Based on these criteria, ELA scores for Model 1 (PS is a unidimensional construct) do contain an acceptable fit (again, see Table 1.5) as TFI; CFI scores are quite close to .90, and RMSEA is .08. The structural equation model tests used to assess the goodness of fit thus revealed that ELA scores, consisting of phonological, onset-rime, and phonemic items can be interpreted as an overall measure of students' ability to discriminate large and small sound units and that their ability to do so is a singular, or unidimensional, ability of PS (Figure 1.3).

ELA ASSESSMENT AND DIRECTIONS

TEACHER IMPLEMENTATION

The ELA is simply an assessment, for both sound and words, that comes with a toolbox for teaching exactly where the student needs instruction. Here is a walk-through of how this works in the form of an example. Our student is "Lucy," and she is in any grade between K and 2, let's say (remember, literacy skill does not exactly correlate with literacy ability based upon chronological age—or grade level, for that matter—and if the student has exceptionalities, the grade can be between K and 8).

Teacher (in a quiet corner of the room): "Hi Lucy. Today I am going to play sound games with you so that I can found out exactly what kinds of sounds I need to teach you!"

Lucy: "Okay." (She smiles, perhaps because the teacher set her at ease and indicated that this is a game—since the items are very gamelike).

Teacher (Opens her *ELA and Toolbox* book to page 26, Rhyming with Simple Words!): "I am going to write down today's date and your name. First, to help get you ready I am going to give you a practice question." (Teacher reads the practice question above). "Okay. Here we go! Do pat and mat rhyme?"

Lucy: "Yes."
The teacher and Lucy keep moving along. Lucy gets above six correct on "Rhyming with Simple Words, Simple Sounds, and Word Count." But then, on "Gluing Words Together," she gets five out of ten correct.

Teacher: "Very good job, Lucy! Now we are going to play more games. The games we are going to play …"

Teacher turns to page 257 to the section labeled "Toolbox for Teaching Using Assessment Results" and specifically to the "Gluing Words Together" instructional game.

Teacher: "Lucy. We are going to play 'Gluing Words Together,' which is a game that makes you hear sounds really well!"

Teacher proceeds to play "Gluing Words Together" with Lucy. After a few sessions with Lucy playing this game, the teacher is ready to assess her again. Only now she will start "Gluing Words Together" and use the second version of that assessment, entitled "Gluing Words Together-2" on page 29 (note that the multiple versions of the same assessments are so that the students do not gain familiarity with the items so that the results are reliable and valid).

At this point, the teacher is going to thus assess Lucy again, and this can occur periodically throughout the year, depending on the student, at least once a month. So now the teacher will do the second assessment starting with "Gluing Words Together," and she won't stop the assessment until Lucy get less than six correct on a form. Where Lucy gets less than six, the teacher will stop, go to the instructional game with the same name as the assessment form, and play the game for teaching and reinforcement. Then the cycle of assessment begins again.

The assessment is no longer needed when students complete all items, ending with "Word Play" starting on page 154, with six or more correct. At this point they will need more advanced morphological instruction with the general literacy curriculum of vocabulary, word identification, and comprehension.

WHAT IS PHONOLOGICAL AWARENESS—SOUND DISCRIMINATION

STUDYING SOUNDS LEADS TO ACHIEVEMENT IN PHONICS AND READING

Phonological Awareness (PA) is the ability to discern both individual sounds within words and the sound of whole words. PA exists on a continuum of skills from easy to difficult. (See examples of PA subskills below.)

Each PA subskill leads to success on the next skill, so teaching the exact PA skill a student needs will enable them to eventually acquire all of the PA skills they need for them to experience success in phonics, a key early reading skill and the foundation for decoding unfamiliar words in text.

Examples of PA sub skills are:

Phonological "big unit" whole-word sounds

1   *Rhyming with Simple Words!* Rhyme: Do hat and cat rhyme? (yes)

2   *Simple Sounds!* Alliteration: Do all three words start with the same sound: bat, ball, small? (yes)

3   *Word Count!* Words: How many words do you count in this sentence: the man went home? (4)

4   *Gluing Words Together!* Syllables: If you take "pig" out of "piglet," what do you have? (let)

5   *Use Your Glue Again—Beginning Sound to Ending Sound!* Onsets and Rimes: What word do these sounds put together make: b-it? (bit)

Phonemic "individual" sounds that are also inside words

1   *Find the Sound!* Isolation: What sound do you hear at the beginning of love, Lou and Lacy? (l)

2   *Find the Same Sound!* Identification: What is the same sound in the following words: cat, bite, lit? (t)

3   *Which Word Belongs!* Categorization: Which word does not belong: hat, cat, bap? (bap)

4   *Word Making Machine!* Blending: What word can you make from the following sounds: k, i, t? (kit)

5   *Sound Count!* Segmenting: How many sounds do you hear in /s/ /i/ /p/? (3)

6   *Remove the Sound!* Phoneme manipulation: Say "par." Now say "par" without the /p/. (ar)

WHAT IS MORPHOLOGICAL AWARENESS—WORD PARTS
STUDYING WORD PARTS INCREASES READING ACHIEVEMENT

Examples of MA sub skills are:

1   *Build the Word with Patterns!* Word Analogy: Listen: "hush, hushed, push." (pushed)

2   *Word Part Remover!* Affix Identification: Say the word "bats." Now make it a shorter word. (bat)

3   *Gluing Word Parts!* Production of Multimorphemic Words: Say "re." Now say "kit." Put them together. (rekit)

4   *Finish the Sentence!* Sentence Analogy: That ball is so bally. That wall is so (wally).

5   *Word Play!* Defining Pseudo Words: The basketball player undunked the ball. (she didn't dunk it)

ELA Connections to Standards

In order to discuss the alignment of these two important literacy components, a new phrase is utilized. The "Next Generation State Standards" phrase encompasses all state standards incorporating the Common Core State Standards (CCSS) within the individual state standards. The alignment tables below do reference the CCSS so that states can determine how state-specific stand

ALIGNMENT INTRODUCTION

The CCSS exist as a cooperative effort between the National Governors Association and the Council of Chief State School Officers. These standards are potentially the most exciting because states in our nation will basically expect all children to know and be able to accomplish the same skills—an exciting venture! However, during the very lengthy process of writing the standards, the focus was on the transition from high school to college and career. With this focus, the emphasis on the interplay between all language systems (phonology, orthography, morphology, syntax, semantics, pragmatics, etymology, and discourse) as students learn to read, write, speak, and listen was somewhat disguised. The interplay of these language systems is crucial to early literacy development in order to grow students to independent reading and writing.

The CCSS leave much to the discretion of states, districts, schools, and educators related to the foundational reading skills as well as language skills. With a tremendous emphasis on "close reading" so that students exit grade twelve ready for college and career academic reading and writing, the requisite language skills are almost an afterthought within the CCSS. These requisite and foundational language skills are necessary for students to read and write at increasingly sophisticated levels across the grade levels. Moats (2012) argues that the CCSS "obfuscates important relationships among word recognition, spelling, fluency, and comprehension....For example, from the standards document, a reader cannot learn that speech sound blending supports word recognition, that spelling supports vocabulary, that understanding morphology speeds word recognition, or that oral language capacities are the underpinning of written language" (p. 33). Thus, it behooves educators to fully understand the mutuality of these important language systems in order to "read between the lines" of the CCSS to ensure that students can access text in order to participate in "close reading"—the very goal of the CCSS.

Since the CCSS doesn't provide the emphasis on these important and foundational skills, educators must assess and provide instruction to ensure that students possess these skills.

Assessing students' individual skills related to phonological and morphological awareness provides educators with the data necessary to provide instruction based on students' needs. Instruction is matched to gaps in student knowledge using teacher-directed, systematic, explicit instruction that is based on the continuum of development for each language component. Phonological awareness and morphological awareness are hugely important foundational skills to put students on a trajectory of successful reading and writing that ultimately results in accessing text to complete that "close reading" and academic-specific writing necessary for college and career attainment.

Tables 1.6–1.9 provide alignment of phonological and morphological awareness to the CCSS.

Table 1.6. Kindergarten Alignment[3].

KINDERGARTEN	PHONOLOGICAL AWARENESS CCSS ALIGNMENT	MORPHOLOGICAL AWARENESS CCSS ALIGNMENT
Sound Discrimination-Phonological Awareness CCSS Reading Standards: Foundational Skills (K–5) Standard 2: Demonstrate understanding of spoken words, syllables, and sounds (phonemes). **Word Parts Knowledge-Morphological Awareness** CCSS Language Standards (K–5) Vocabulary Acquisition and Use Standard 4: Determine or clarify the meaning of unknown and multiple-meaning words and phrases based on kindergarten reading and content.	a. Recognize and produce rhyming words.	Identify new meanings for familiar words and apply them accurately (e.g., knowing *duck* is a bird and learning the verb *to duck*).
	b. Count, pronounce, blend, and segment syllables in a word.	Use the most frequently occurring inflections and affixes (e.g., *-ed, -s, re-, un-, pre-, -ful, -less*) as a clue to the meaning of an unknown word.
	c. Blend and segment onset and rimes of single-syllable spoken words.	
	d. Isolate and pronounce the initial, medial vowel, and final sounds (phonemes) in three-phoneme (consonant-vowel-consonant or CVC) words.* (This does not include CVCs ending with /l/, /r/, or /x/.)	
	e. Add or substitute individual sounds (phonemes) in simple one-syllable words to make new words.	

3   Adapted from: http://www.corestandards.org/ELA-Literacy/RF/K/. Copyright © by Common Core State Standards Initiative.

Table 1.7. First Grade Alignment[4].

GRADE ONE	PHONOLOGICAL AWARENESS CCSS ALIGNMENT	MORPHOLOGICAL AWARENESS CCSS ALIGNMENT
Sound Discrimination-Phonological Awareness CCSS Reading Standards: Foundational Skills (K–5) Standard 2: Demonstrate understanding of spoken words, syllables, and sounds (phonemes). **Word Parts Knowledge-Morphological Awareness** CCSS Language Standards (K–5) Vocabulary Acquisition and Use Standard 4: Determine or clarify the meaning of unknown and multiple-meaning words and phrases based on grade 1 reading and content, choosing flexibly from an array of strategies.	a. Distinguish long from short vowel sounds in spoken single-syllable words.	Use sentence-level context as a clue to the meaning of a word or phrase.
	b. Orally produce single-syllable words by blending sounds (phonemes) including consonant blends.	Use frequently occurring affixes as a clue to the meaning of a word.
	c. Isolate and pronounce initial, medial vowel, and final sounds (phonemes) in spoken single-syllable words.	Identify frequently occurring root words (e.g., *look*) and their inflectional forms (e.g., *looks, looked, looking*).
	d. Segment spoken single-syllable words into their complete sequence of individual sounds (phonemes).	

Table 1.8. Second Grade Alignment[5].

GRADE TWO	MORPHOLOGICAL AWARENESS CCSS ALIGNMENT
Sound Discrimination-Phonological Awareness None **Word Parts Knowledge-Morphological Awareness** CCSS Language Standards (K–5) Vocabulary Acquisition and Use Standard 4: Determine or clarify the meaning of unknown and multiple-meaning words and phrases based on grade 2 reading and content, choosing flexibly from an array of strategies.	a. Use sentence-level context as a clue to the meaning of a word or phrase.
	b. Determine the meaning of the new word formed when a known prefix is added to a known word (e.g., *happy/unhappy, tell/retell*).
	c. Use a known root word as a clue to the meaning of an unknown word with the same root (e.g., *addition, additional*).
	d. Use knowledge of the meaning of individual words to predict the meaning of compound words (e.g., *birdhouse, lighthouse, housefly; bookshelf, notebook, bookmark*).
	e. Use glossaries and beginning dictionaries, both print and digital, to determine or clarify the meaning of words and phrases.

---

4   Adapted from: http://www.corestandards.org/ELA-Literacy/RF/1/. Copyright © by Common Core State Standards Initiative.

5   Adapted from: http://www.corestandards.org/ELA-Literacy/L/2/. Copyright © by Common Core State Standards Initiative.

Table 1.9. Third Grade Alignment[6].

GRADE THREE	MORPHOLOGICAL AWARENESS CCSS ALIGNMENT
Sound Discrimination-Phonological Awareness None **Word Parts Knowledge-Morphological Awareness** CCSS Language Standards (K–5) Vocabulary Acquisition and Use Standard 4: Determine or clarify the meaning of unknown and multiple-meaning words and phrases based on grade 3 reading and content, choosing flexibly from an array of strategies.	a. Use sentence-level context as a clue to the meaning of a word or phrase. b. Determine the meaning of the new word formed when a known affix is added to a known word (e.g., *agreeable/disagreeable, comfortable/uncomfortable, care/careless, heat/preheat*). c. Use a known root word as a clue to the meaning of an unknown word with the same root (e.g., *company, companion*). d. Use glossaries and beginning dictionaries, both print and digital, to determine or clarify the precise meaning of key words and phrases.

ASSESS AND THEN TEACH! DIRECTIONS FOR ASSESSMENT OF SOUND DISCRIMINATION (PHONOLOGICAL AWARENESS)

The assessor administers the Sound Discrimination Assessment individually to students. The assessment is made up of eleven sections with ten items per page and seven versions of each section. The eleven sections are Rhyming with Simple Words, Simple Sounds, Word Count, Gluing Words Together, Use Your Glue Again—Beginning Sound to Ending Sound, Find the Sound, Find the Same Sound, Which Word Belongs, Word-Making Machine, Sound Count, and Remove the Sound.

IMPORTANT INFORMATION ABOUT THE ASSESSMENT OF SOUND DISCRIMINATION

Each section has a practice test item. The assessor will begin with the practice item and make sure the student knows what is expected of him/her. The assessor will then read the test items to the student and wait for a response. The answer for each test item is listed in

---

6   Adapted from: http://www.corestandards.org/ELA-Literacy/L/3/. Copyright © by Common Core State Standards Initiative.

parentheses. If the student answers correctly, place a check mark in the box to the right of the text item. Any comments or notes the assessor has can be recorded in the section on the left of the document entitled "Assessor Comments." If the student misses three or more of the test items on that page, the assessment should be concluded. If the student scores six or more answers correctly, then the assessor is to move on to the next page of the assessment. Continue with this process until the student does not score six or better on a section of the assessment.

HELP:
Student answers at least six correct—*GO* to the next assessment!
Student answers fewer than six correct—*STOP* and go to the game in the "Toolbox for Teaching Using Assessment Results."

Rhyming with Simple Words—In the beginning stages of phonological awareness, we often begin with teaching students about rhyming words. This section addresses simple rhyming words by stating two words and then asking the student if both of the words rhyme. For example, the practice item reminds the student to listen carefully and then asks the student, "Do pot and lot rhyme?" Remind the student that they are listening to the rhyme of the words, not the beginning sound of the words.

Simple Sounds—Recognizing sound is a vital part of phonological awareness, and it is important that we afford students the opportunities to play with sound. The simple sound section allows student to explore the beginning sounds of words. The practice item requires the student to listen carefully to the beginning sound of three words. For example, the practice item states, "I am going to say three words: mitt; mat; mud. Do all three words start with the same sound?" Remind the student that they are specifically listening to only the beginning sound of the three words.

Word Count—Recognizing that there are separate words in sentences is also a stage of phonological awareness. The word count section calls for the student to listen to how many words are in each stated sentence. For example, the practice item asks, "How many words are in this list? The dog ran." Be sure to speak clearly and specifically while moving through the word count section.

Gluing Words Together—Blending words, segmenting words, and removing words requires the student to perform three separate skills. The practice item states, "Blend together the words that you hear (basket; ball to basketball), segment (bedroom to bed; room), or remove a word (aircraft without air; craft). Remind the student that blending calls for putting two words or sounds together, segmenting requires the separation of two words or sounds, and removing requires taking away a word or sound.

Use Your Glue Again—Beginning Sound to Ending Sound—As we move through activities that involve phonological awareness, it is key that students are afforded the opportunity to blend sounds together. This section calls for the student to blend two sounds together to make a word. For example, the practice item states "Blend the following sounds: /b/- /ig/." Remind the student that they are to listen to the two separate sounds and then push those sounds together to make a word.

Find the Sound—Listening to the sound at the begging, middle, and end of words also calls for the student to find specific sounds. The practice item asks, "What sound do you hear at the beginning of dig; dot; dip?" As the assessor moves through this section, the questions then change their focus to the ending sounds of words. An example of this type of question would be "What do you hear at the end of cat; sat; rat?" The final questions in this section address the middle sound of words. These questions ask the student, "What do you hear in the middle of these words?"

Find the Same Sound—This section calls for the student to find the same sound in a list of three words. The practice item states, "What sound do you hear in this list of words: lip, lean, lad?" Halfway through the section, the task moves to recognizing the same ending sounds of the three stated words. An example of this type of question is "What same sound do you hear in this list of words: put, hat, mitt?" The end of this section focuses on the middle sound of the three given words. For example, "What same sound do you hear in this list of words: lip, sit, hid?"

Which Words Belong?—In this section, students must find the word that does not belong. This section addresses beginning sounds, middle sounds, and ending sounds. For example, the practices item calls for the student to answer, "Which of the following words does not belong: jump, jar, mar?" Remind the student that they are specifically listening for the word that does not belong because of its sound.

Word-Making Machine—This section requires the student to listen to a list of letter sounds and then put the sounds together to form a word. For example, the practice test items states, "What word can you make from putting together the following sounds: /p/ /a/ /t/?" As the student moves through the assessment, the amount of sounds increases in number.

Sound Count—Students must recognize that sounds make up words. This section asks the student to listen to the stated sounds and then state how many sounds are in the word. The practice test item states, "How many sounds do you hear in the following word: /h/ /a/ /t/ ? As the section continues, the amount of sounds increases in number.

Remove the Sound—The final section of the Phonological Assessment calls for the student to remove a sound in each stated word. For example, the assessor would state, "Say 'car' without the /c/ at the beginning." As the student moves through the assessment, the task gets more difficult. For example, the assessor would state, "Say *bake* with a /c/ instead of a /b/."

GRADE LEVELS AND RANGES AND STUDENTS WITH EXCEPTIONALITIES

GRADES PRE-K–3 AND FOR STUDENTS WITH READING DIFFICULTY

Procedures: Tell the student that you are going to learn more about him or her and specifically learn about their knowledge of sounds and words. For each question type, you read the example outlined at the top of the page. Each page is its own subskill. Proceed to question the individual student in a quiet area.

SCORING TO IDENTIFY TEACHING LEVEL

Once the student cannot get six or more answers correct (out of ten), stop and go to the Toolbox section of this book and teach that skill.

SOUND DISCRIMINATION ASSESSMENT VERSIONS 1–7

Once the student cannot get six or more answers correct (out of ten), stop and go to the Toolbox section of this book and teach that skill.

ASSESS AND THEN TEACH! DIRECTIONS FOR ASSESSMENT OF WORD PARTS STUDY (MORPHOLOGICAL AWARENESS)

OVERVIEW

The Word Part portion of the assessment is administered individually to students by the evaluator. The assessment is made up of five sections with ten items per page and ten versions of each section. The sections have brief directions and a test practice item. The evaluator will begin with the practice item and make sure the student knows what is expected of him/her. After making sure the student understands the practice item, the evaluator will read the test items to the student, wait for a response, and then place a check mark by each item that is answered correctly. If the student misses four or more of the test items on that page, that section testing is over, and the next one begins. Continue with this process until all five sections have been scored.

> **HELP:**
> **Student answers at least six correct—*GO* to the next assessment!**
> **Student answers fewer than six correct—*STOP* and go to the game in the "Toolbox for Teaching Using Assessment Results."**

THE FIVE SECTIONS

1 Build the Word with Patterns!

2 Word Part Remover!

3 Gluing Word Parts!

4 Finish the Sentence!

5 Word Play!

DIRECTIONS FOR EACH SECTION

Build the Word with Patterns!—There is a set of four words by each number. The evaluator should repeat the first three words clearly and distinctively, then wait for the student to give the final word. The answer is in bold-faced type. If the student answers correctly, place a check mark in the box to the right of the test item. Any comments or notes the evaluator has can be recorded in the section on the left called Evaluator comments.

Word Part Remover!—Read the pseudoword for each item and wait for the student to give you the shortened version of the pseudoword, which has had the affixes removed. The answer is in bold-faced type. Mark the correct responses with a check mark in the box on the right. Again, the test section continues until the student has missed half or more of the test items on that page. When that number has been reached, move to the next section.

Gluing Word Parts!—Slowly, say the parts of the word, and the student will repeat the parts. The student then combines the parts to make a real word or pseudoword. The answers are in parentheses at the end of the item line. Mark the correct responses in the boxes, to the right. Stop this section when half or more of the items are missed. Then, move to the next section.

Finish the Sentence!—Read the first two sentences, the first sentence of the next set, and then part of the next sentence, waiting for the student to complete it. The student should give you the answer that is in bold-faced type at the end of the test item. Mark the correct responses with a check mark in the box and continue until half or more items are missed in this section. Move to the next section and begin.

Word Play!—Read the sentence containing pseudowords with real affixes for the student. The student will tell what the sentence means by using the prefix meanings. The student should offer a negative response. Mark the correct responses with a check mark in the box and continue until half or more items are missed in this section.

GRADE LEVELS AND RANGES AND STUDENTS WITH EXCEPTIONALITIES GRADES 2–6

Procedures: Tell the student that you are going to learn more about him or her and specifically learn about their knowledge of sounds and words. For each question type, you read the example outlined at the top of the page. Each page is its own subskill. Proceed to question the individual student in a quiet area.

SCORING TO IDENTIFY TEACHING LEVEL

Once the student cannot get six or more answers correct (out of ten), stop and go to the Toolbox section of this book and teach that skill.

WORD PART KNOWLEDGE ASSESSMENT VERSION S 1–7

Once the student cannot get six or more answers correct (out of ten), stop and go to the Toolbox section of this book and teach that skill.

REFERENCES

Graney, S., &   Shinn, M. (2005). The effects of reading curriculum-based measurement(R-CBM) teacher feedback in general education classrooms. *School Psychology Review*, 34, 184-201.

Guskey, T.R. (2003). How classroom assessments can improve learning. *Educational Leadership*, (5), 60, pp. 2-18.

Moats, L. C. (2012). Reconciling the Common Core Standards with reading research. Perspectives on Language and Literacy. Washington, D. C.: American Federation of Teachers.

National Reading Panel (2000). Teaching children to read: An evidence-based assessment of the scientific research literature on reading and its implications for reading instruction [on-line]. Available: http://www.nichd.nih.gov/publications/nrp/smallbook.htm.

Overholt, R., & Szabocsik (2013). Leadership content knowledge for literacy: Connecting literacy teachers and their principals. *The Clearing House: A Journal of Educational Strategies, Issues and Ideas*, 2, 86.

Popham, W.J. (1995). *Classroom assessment: What teachers need to know*. Needham Heights, MA: Allyn & Bacon.

Torgesen, J.K., & Bryant, B. (2004). *Test of Phonological Awareness*, 2nd Edition: PLUS (TOPA-2+) [Complete kit]. Austin, TX: PRO-ED.

SIMPLE SOUNDS! -1-

date	student	teacher	
Skill Focus: ALLITERATION			**Correct = √**
Practice: *"I am going to say three words: mitt; mat; mud. Do all three words start with the same sound?"* - (pause)- *"Yes."*			
-1- (/d/) Do all three of these words start with the same sound: dog, dig, bag? (No).			
-2- (/b/) Do all three of these words start with the same sound: big, bed, bad? (Yes).			
-3- (/c/) Do all three of these words start with the same sound: cat, cup, can? (Yes).			
-4- (/n/) Do all three of these words start with the same sound: nap, nod, mop? (No).			
-5-(/sn/) Do all three of these words start with the same sound: snap, snail, snout? (Yes).			
-6- (/cl/) Do all three of these words start with the same sound: cloud, clown, bark? (No).			
-7- (/bl) Do all three of these words start with the same sound: black, blue, bland? (Yes).			
-8- sh/ Do all three of these words start with the same sound: sheep, ship, shine? (Yes).			
-9- /ch/ Do all three of these words start with the same sound: cheap, choose, could? (No).			
-10- oi/ Do all three of these words start with the same sound: oil, oink, oyster? (Yes)			

WORD COUNT! -1-			
date	student	teacher	

Skill Focus: WORDS IN SENTENCES	Correct = √
Practice: "How many words are in this list? He hit the ball." (4)	
-1- How many words are in this list? The dog ran home. (4)	
-2- How many words are in this list? Tom is tall. (3)	
-3- How many words are in this list? Kim walked to school. (4)	
-4- How many words are in this list? The cat chased the mouse. (5)	
-5-How many words are in this list? My arm is broken. (4)	
-6- How many words are in this list? Sit down to eat dinner. (5)	
-7- How many words are in this list? Mom cooked eggs, bacon, and biscuits. (6)	
-8- How many words are in this list? The bird flew off the roof. (6)	
-9- How many words are in this list? The green frog jumped in the muddy puddle. (8)	
-10- How many words are in this list? Look, I am jumping very high! (6)	

GLUING WORDS TOGETHER! -1-			
date	student	teacher	

Skill Focus: SYLLABLES	Correct = √
Practice: "Blend together the words that you hear (basket; ball to basketball), segment (bedroom to bed; room), or remove a word (aircraft without air; craft)."	
-1- Listen to these two words: gem; stone. Say the entire word together (gemstone).	
-2- Listen to these two words: hair; cut. Say the entire word together (haircut).	
-3- Listen to these two words: foot; ball. Say the entire word together (football).	
-4- Listen to these two words: gold; fish. Say the entire word together (goldfish).	
-5- What two words do you hear in grandparent? (grand; parent)	
-6- What two words do you hear in jackpot? (jack; pot)	
-7- What two words to you hear in ladybug? (lady; bug)	
-8- If you take moon out of moonbeam, what do you have left? (beam)	
-9- If you take night out of nightstand, what do you have left? (stand)	
-10- If you take ball out of meatball, what do you have left? (meat)	

INFORMED TEACHING

USE YOUR GLUE AGAIN—BEGINNING SOUND TO ENDING SOUND! -1-

date	student	teacher	
Skill Focus: ONSET AND RIME			**Correct = √**
Practice: *Blend the following sounds: /b/- /ig/." - (pause) - "big."*			
-1- Blend the following sounds: /s/-/at/. (sat)			
-2- Blend the following sounds: /n/- /ap/. (nap)			
-3- Blend the following sounds: /t/-/on/. (ton)			
-4- Blend the following sounds: /f/ -/at/. (fat)			
-5- Blend the following sounds: /m/-/oon/. (moon)			
-6- Blend the following sounds: /h/- /and/. (hand)			
-7- Blend the following sounds: /s/-/alt/. (salt)			
-8- Blend the following sounds: /bl /-/ack/. (black)			
-9- Blend the following sounds: /fr/-/og/. (frog)			
-10- Blend the following sounds: /st/- /aller/. (staller)			

FIND THE SOUND! -1-

date	student	teacher	
Skill Focus: ISOLATION			**Correct = √**
Practice: *"What sound do you hear at the beginning of dig; dot; dip?" - (pause)- "/d/"* (sound not letter)			
-1- What do you hear at the **beginning** of pat; pick; pot? (/p/)			
-2- What do you hear at the **beginning** of back; bear; big? (/b/)			
-3- What do you hear at the **beginning** of nip; nod; neck? (/n/)			
-4- What do you hear at the **beginning** of lid; lock; loan? (l)			
-5-What do you hear at the **end** of cat; sat; rat? (t)			
-6- What do you hear at the **end** of face; place; case? /s/			
-7- What do you hear at the **end of** load; mode; toad? /d/			
-8- What do you hear in the **middle** of sip; tip; nip? /i/			
-9- What do you hear in the **middle** of mutt; put; cut? /u/			
-10- What do you hear in the **middle of** coat; moat; boat? /oa/ (Pronounce complex vowel sound of /oa/ as long vowel o).			

FIND THE SAME SOUND! -1-

date	student	teacher	

Skill Focus: IDENTITY — Correct = √

Practice: *"What same sound do you hear in this list of words? lip, lean, lad?"* -(pause)- *"/l/"* (sound not letter)

-1- What same sound do you hear in this list of words: nap, not, Nick? (/n/)	
-2- What same sound do you hear in this list of words: lad, lip, luck? (/l/)	
-3- What same sound do you hear in this list of words: dark, dip, dog? (/d/)	
-4- What same sound do you hear in this list of words: umbrella, under, us? (/u/)	
-5- What same sound do you hear in this list of words: put, hat, mitt? (/t/)	
-6- What same sound do you hear in this list of words: sad, could, dud? (/d/)	
-7- What same sound do you hear in this list of words: Tom, ham, dim? (/m/)	
-8- What same sound do you hear in this list of words: lip, sit, hid? (/i/) (short i)	
-9- What same sound do you hear in this list of words: pot, knob, fox? (/o/) (short o)	
-10- What same sound do you hear in this list of words: pad, sat, rack? (/a/) (short a)	

WHICH WORD BELONGS? -1-

date	student	teacher	

Skill Focus: CATEGORIZATION — Correct = √

Practice: *"Which of the following words does not belong: jump, jar, mar?"* - (pause) - *"mar."*

-1- Which of the following words does not belong: sick; David; sad? (David)	
-2- Which of the following words does not belong: lad; lick; cake? (cake)	
-3- Which of the following words does not belong: sud; kick; kite? (sud)	
-4- Which of the following words does not belong: tack; back; nap? (nap)	
-5- Which of the following words does not belong: pull; shoe; fill? (shoe)	
-6- Which of the following words does not belong: tot; men; pin? (tot)	
-7- Which of the following words does not belong: pill; mull; note? (note)	
-8- Which of the following words does not belong: ran; mutt; bub? (ran)	
-9- Which of the following words does not belong: pat; lim; tam? (lim)	
-10- Which of the following words does not belong: sip, hit, tock? (tock)	

79

INFORMED TEACHING

WORD-MAKING MACHINE! -1-

date	student	teacher	
Skill Focus: BLENDING			**Correct = √**
Practice: *"What word can you make from putting together the following sounds: /p/ /a/ /t/ ?"* - (pause)- *"pat."*			
-1- What word can you make from putting together the following sounds: /p/ /u/ /ll/ ? (pull)			
-2- What word can you make from putting together the following sounds: /s/ /i/ /n/ ? (sin)			
-3- What word can you make from putting together the following sounds: /t/ /a/ /p/ ? (tap)			
-4- What word can you make from putting together the following sounds: /s/ /a/ /n/ /d/ ? (sand)			
-5- What word can you make from putting together the following sounds: /l/ /o/ /t/ /s/ ? (lots)			
-6- What word can you make from putting together the following sounds: /s/ /n/ /a/ /p/ ? (snap)			
-7- What word can you make from putting together the following sounds: /p/ /a/ /s/ /t/ ? (past)			
-8- What word can you make from putting together the following sounds: /m/ /a/ /k/ /r/ ? (maker)			
-9- What word can you make from putting together the following sounds: /t/ /i/ /n/ /t/ /r/ ? (tinter)			
-10- What word can you make from putting together the following sounds: /s/ /l/ /ee/ /p/ /r/ ? (sleeper)			

RHYMING WITH SIMPLE WORDS! - 1-

date	student	teacher	
Skill Focus: RHYME			**Correct = √**
Practice: *"The two words that I am going to say may or may not rhyme, so listen carefully. Do lot and pot rhyme?"* - (pause)- *"Yes".*			
-1- Do pat and mat rhyme? (Yes)			
-2- Do sit and bit rhyme? (Yes)			
-3- Do car and rat rhyme? (No)			
-4- Do lap and sip rhyme? (No)			
-5- Do land and hand rhyme? (Yes)			
-6- Do tend and bend rhyme? (Yes)			
-7- Do bake and bike rhyme? (No)			
-8- Do bippert and mippert rhyme? (Yes)			
-9- Do lupper and lipper rhyme? (No)			
-10- Do pilner and dilner rhyme? (Yes)			

SOUND COUNT! -1-			
date	student	teacher	
Skill Focus: SEGMENTING			Correct = √

Practice: *"How many sounds do you hear in the following word? /h/ /a/ /t/ ?"* - (pause) - *"three."*

-1- How many sounds do you hear in the following word: /j/ /a/ /m/ ? (jam) (3)	
-2- How many sounds do you hear in the following word: /o/ /n/? (on) (2)	
-3- How many sounds do you hear in the following word: /n/ /i/ /p/? (nip) (3)	
-4- How many sounds do you hear in the following word: /s/ /c/ /a/ /b/? (scab) (4)	
-5- How many sounds do you hear in the following word: /c/ /l/ /a/ /p/? (clap) (4)	
-6- How many sounds do you hear in the following word: /b/ /u/ /m/ /p/? (bump)(4)	
-7- How many sounds do you hear in the following word: /d/ /a/ /r/ /k/? (dark) (4)	
-8- How many sounds do you hear in the following word: /r/ /u/ /p/ /r/ /t/? (ruppert) (5)	
-9- How many sounds do you hear in the following word: /b/ /a/ /k/ /r/? (baker) (4)	
-10- How many sounds do you hear in the following word: /s/ /a/ /p/ /r/ /z/? (sapers) (5)	

INFORMED TEACHING

REMOVE THE SOUND! -1-			
date	student	teacher	
Skill Focus: MANIPULATION			**Correct = √**
Practice: "*Say 'car' without the /c/ at the beginning. You would say …*" -(pause)- "*/r/.*"			
-1- Say *hat* without the /h/ (at).			
-2- Say *mit* without the /m/ (it).			
-3- Say *at* without the /a/ (t).			
-4- Say *skit* without the /t/ (ski).			
-5-Say *cast* without the /s/ (cat).			
-6- Say *hunt* without the /n/ (hut).			
-7- Say *jist* without the /s/ (jit).			
-8- Say *at* with a /m/ at the beginning (mat).			
-9- Say *it* with a /p/ at the beginning (pit).			
-10- Say *bake* with a /c/ instead of a /b/ (cake).			

BUILD THE WORD WITH PATTERNS! SECTION 1 -V1-			
date	student	teacher	
Skill Focus: Affixation			**Correct = √**
Directions for Build the Word with Patterns: Slowly repeat the first two words, pause, then say the third word. Ask the student to supply the final word to complete the set. The answer is in bold for each item. Mark the correct response with a check mark in the box. Be sure to use the practice item first to help the student understand what is expected. Begin the test and continue until the student misses half or more of the items on the page, then move to the next section.			
Practice: "*Listen: gush: gushed. Listen again: tush. What is next?*" (tushed)			
-1- mesh: meshed—besh: **beshed**			
-2- ram: rams—bim: **bims**			
-3- bake: baking—sake: **saking**			
-4- mop: mopper—fop: **fopper**			
-5- catch: catcher—gatch: **gatcher**			
-6- bats: bat—dats: **dat**			
-7- honor: dishonor—continue: **discontinue**			
-8- unreal: real—just: **unjust**			
-9- plain: plainly—bate: **bately**			
-10- music: musician—fusic: *fuscian*			

WORD PART REMOVER! SECTION 2 -V1-			
date	student	teacher	
Skill Focus: Affix Deletion			Correct = √

Directions for Word Part Remover: Read the pseudoword for each item and wait for the student to give you the shortened version of the pseudoword that has had the affixes removed. The answer is in bold. Mark the correct responses with a check mark in the box on the right. Continue until the student has missed half or more of the test items on the page, then move to the next section.

Practice: *"Repeat: binking. Remove the affix and say the shortened word."* (bink)

-1- zins: **zin**	
-2- zilled: **zill**	
-3- dacking: **dack**	
-4- zainly: **zain**	
-5- fetter: **fet**	
-6- macked: **mack**	
-7- lishes: **lish**	
-8- dunning: **dun**	
-9- maver: **mave**	
-10- taction: **tact**	

INFORMED TEACHING

GLUING WORD PARTS! SECTION 3 -V1-			
date	student	teacher	

Skill Focus: Combining Word Parts	Correct = √

Directions for Gluing Word Parts: The evaluator will slowly say the parts of the word, and the student will repeat the parts. Then the student combines the parts to make a real word or pseudoword. The answers are in parentheses at the end of the item line. Mark the correct responses in the boxes to the right. Stop when half or more of the items are missed, then move to the next section.

Practice: *"Repeat after me: 're' and 'do.' Combined, it is* (redo)."

-1- "Repeat after me: 're' and 'shape.' Combined, it is (reshape)."	
-2- "Repeat after me: 'un' and 'happy.' Combined, it is (unhappy)."	
-3- "Repeat after me: 'in' and 'visible.' Combined, it is (invisible)."	
-4- "Repeat after me: 'dis' and 'able.' Combined, it is (disable)."	
-5- "Repeat after me: 'pre' and 'treat.' Combined, it is (pretreat)."	
-6- "Repeat after me: 'mis' and 'trust.' Combined, it is (mistrust)."	
-7- "Repeat after me: 'trust' + 'ing.' Combined it is (trusting)."	
-8- "Repeat after me: 'help' and 'less.' Combined, it is (helpless)."	
-9- "Repeat after me: 'rest' and 'ful.' Combined, it is (restful)."	
-10- "Repeat after me: 'ex' and 'port' and 'er.' Combined, it is (exporter)."	

FINISH THE SENTENCE! SECTION 4 -V1-			
date	student	teacher	

Skill Focus: Morpheme Pattern Match	Correct = √

Directions for Finish the Sentence: The evaluator will read the first two sentences, the first sentence of the next set, and then part of the next sentence, waiting for the student to complete it. The student should give you the answer that is in bold in the last sentence. Mark the correct responses in the boxes to the right. Stop when half or more of the items are missed, then move to the next section.

Practice: "Listen to the first two sentences. Now listen again and see if you can finish the sentence when I stop. 'The jogger jogs: The speeder speeds.' 'The shopper shops: The singer sings.'"

-1- The baby wet his diaper: The baby wets his diaper. The man put the paper down: The man **puts** the paper down.	
-2- Rita talked to Dale: Rita talks to Dale. Sophie laughed at the kitten: Sophie **laughs** at the kitten.	
-3- Bob was marked: Bob was unmarked. Sally was zacked: Sally was **unzacked**.	
-4- The robber robs: The scrubber scrubs. The hugger hugs: The digger **digs**.	
-5- The man covered the grill: The man covers the grill. The man cleaned the pool: The man **cleans** the pool.	
-6- Ron's car is fancy: Dak's car is fancier. Tameka is pretty: Simone is **prettier**.	
-7- Martha clears the walkway: Martha is clearing the walkway. Phil bangs the door: Phil is **banging** the door.	
-8- The salt is salty: The grit is gritty. The butter is buttery: The cream is **creamy**.	
-9- Meg is unwilling to work: Meg can be very unwilling to work. The lady is unkind: The lady is behaving **unkindly**.	
-10- Lee's dog had matched eyes: Ray's dog had mismatched eyes. The boy learned the math equation: The girl **mislearned** the math equation.	

WORD PLAY! SECTION 5 -V1-			
date	student	teacher	
Skill Focus: Define Pseudowords			Correct = √

Directions for Word Play: The evaluator will read the sentence containing pseudowords with real affixes. The student will tell what the sentence means by using the prefix meanings and offer a negative response. The answer is in bold at the end of the item. Mark the correct responses in the boxes to the right. Stop when half or more of the items are missed, then move to the next section.

Practice: *"Listen as I read the sentence that has a made-up word and tell me what it means. 'The clown depainted his face, since he already had a big smile.'"* (clown did not paint his face, because he had a big smile)

-1- Ricky was new in the school and was nonfriended. **(no friends because he was new)**	
-2- Cindy unwalks her dog every day, since her friend helps. **(does not walk dog every day because friend helps)**	
-3- Lizards declimbed, only, on the tree branch. **(lizards did not climb only on tree branch)**	
-4- Jeri unfavored the second movie over the first one. **(did not like second movie the most)**	
-5- The computer game was fun to play, but it was depowered. **(liked to play game, but not powered)**	

CREDITS

Interactive Assessment Work-Map

START HERE

1

Directions

For the example assessment above you are now going to "interact" with it as you check off criteria and write brief statements and definitions about its general type and, specifically, its reliability, validity, value and utility technical characteristics. You are encouraged to infer how the assessment might be used in your own teaching if applicable.

2 ✎

How Is the Assessment Administered?

Individual ☐

Group ☐

3

Assessment, Test, Measurement, Evaluation Type

Note that an assessment can contain multiple types and/or degrees of type.

Test ☐ Achievement in what academic area/subject/domain?

Quiz ☐ For reinforcement/application or demonstrated understanding

Survey ☐ Cognitive and/or behavioral

Portfolio ☐ Collection of artifacts for learner demonstration of meeting various criteria and/or understanding

Inventory ☐ Collection of items/prompts for discernment of learning in a comprehensive manner, with all sub-elements of that area included _____

Artifact ☐ Specific evidence to learner demonstration of among various criteria and/or understanding

Exam ☐ Measuring specific content-area aligned to specific learning objectives

Case ☐ A specific unit of analysis or person with defined boundaries

Writing Prompt ☐ A query, question or directive to guide student writing

Content Area Performance/Presentation ☐

Qualities and Characteristics

Check each box that applies and briefly notate how the assessment meets these defined criteria for assessment purpose, making inferences from results and interpreting data.

☐ Static- _____ Dynamic ☐

☐ Developmental

☐ Vertical

☐ Formative _____ Summative ☐

☐ Value for Who/When/How?

-Student ☐
-Teacher ☐
-Parent ☐
-Administrator ☐
-Community ☐

Utility ☐ (Leading to specific Actions) _____

5

4

Reliability and Validity

Reliable ☐

- - - - - - - - - - - - - - - - - - - -

Valid **FOR WHAT PURPOSE?**
Describe assessment features that support the validity type/s identification.

-Face ☐

-Content ☐

-Criterion-related ☐

-Construct ☐

-Concurrent ☐

-Predictive ☐

-Developmental ☐

Interactive Assessment Work-Map developed by M. Mott (2016).

Interactive Assessment Work-Map NOTES

Reliability and Validity Description

6

Reliable ☐

Valid ***FOR WHAT PURPOSE?*** *Describe assessment features that support the validity type/s identification. See information on validity definitions in the Reliability, Validity, Value, and Utility section of this book.*

-Face ☐

-Content ☐

-Criterion-related ☐

-Construct ☐

-Concurrent ☐

-Predictive ☐

-Developmental ☐

Interactive Assessment Work-Map developed by M. Mott (2016).

Interactive Assessment Work-Map NOTES

Value and Utility

Discuss and describe the educational value of the assessment under review. What does it do? Who does it help and how? Why can it inform teaching and learning? Can it inform educational policy and leadership decision making? In what manner?

7

Value for …?

Students ☐
-Content Area
-Cognitive
-Social-Emotional

-Teachers ☐
-Inform Instruction
-Formative
-Summative
-Dynamic

Utility for …?

-Administrators ☐
-Support Supervision Goals and Policy
-Guide Schoolwide Efforts and Programming
-Parents and Community ☐
-Information for Parents on Status of Education

Interactive Assessment Work-Map developed by M. Mott (2016).

Interactive Assessment Work-Map NOTES

Applications to *Your* Professional Practice

8 Given the reliability, validity, value, and utility characteristics of the current assessment under review, discuss and describe how you would apply it in your professional practice. Hypothetically illustrate a reasoned use for the assessment and freely identify its strengths and limitations (validity issues) for making inferences from the results of the assessment for instruction.

Interactive Assessment Work-Map developed by M. Mott (2016).

ASSESSMENT EXAMPLE 2. PHONICS INVENTORY SAMPLE

BACKGROUND

In early reading curriculum and instruction, the teaching of phonics is a core skill developed in grades K–3. Phonics, or "decoding," is a skill that is foundational to word identification and consists of learning sound–symbol correspondences in order to blend sounds together to form words. Sounds, or phonemes, are matched with symbols, or letters, and this represents two language systems at work—phonological and orthographical. The phonological system is the language system where sound is processed at the individual sound unit level (phoneme), syllable, and whole word. The orthographic system is the graphical representation of a language from individual sound-letter units (graphemes) to complex words with multiple graphemes. In phonics instruction, the synthesis of phonological and orthographic processing begins with simple phoneme-grapheme mapping to teach the "alphabetic code."

The developmental continuum of phonics generally moves from:

SKILL CONTINUUM	SOUND—PHONOLOGICAL REPRESENTATION	SYMBOL—ORTHOGRAPHIC REPRESENTATION
Initial consonants	Examples- /b/ /c/ /d/ /f/	b, c, d, f
Final consonants	Examples- /b/ /k/ /n/ /t/	b, ck, k, n, t
Long vowel sounds	Examples- /a/ /e/ /i/ /o/	a_e, a, e, ee, ea, i, ie, y, o, o_e igh
Short medial vowel sounds	/a/ /e/ /i/ /o/ /u/	a, a_e, ea, e, ee, ea, ie, i, igh, ie, y, o, u
Medial consonants	Examples- /b/ /c/ /d/ /f/	b, c, d, f
Advanced vowel generalizations	/i/ /e/	igh, ee
Within-word structure	/ake/	cake, bake, sake, nake, slake
Advanced complex words with morphemes (suffixation) and etymological patterns such as Greek or Latin derivations	/dis/	disengage, disinclined, dismiss

Phonics instruction takes place within the continuum above, moving from easier initial consonants all the way to complex word recognition and identification required of fluent readers who comprehend text.

SURVEYS

- *Names—Capital Letters*
- *Names—Lowercase Letters*
- *Sounds—Vowels*
- *Sounds—Consonants*
- *Diagraphs of Consonants*

WORD READING/PHONETIC DECODING

- *Sounds of Short Vowels*
- *Short Vowels with Consonant Diagraphs*
- *Short Vowels with Consonant Blends*
- *Vowel + "e"*
- *Diphthongs and Diagraphs with Vowels*
- *R & L Controlled*
- *Prefixes*
- *Suffixes*
- *Words with Multiple Syllables*

PHONICS SURVEY

Name:_____Date:_____Score:_____

Directions:

Students should be given this assessment individually. Give the Student's Copy to the students, and the instructor will have the Teacher's Copy. While administering this survey, the teacher will make marks to show which ones the students have answered correctly. For each skill, the teacher will ask these series of questions. Question 1 corresponds with the first box (letter names of capital letters), the second question corresponds to the second box (letter names of lowercase letters), and so forth:

1   What are the **names** of these letters?

2   What are the names of these letters?

3   What **sound** does each of these letters make?

4   What **sound** does each of the pairs of letters make?

5   What **sounds** do each of these letters make? (Encourage the student to think of more than one sound each of the letters makes.)

*If the student cannot read two or more of the real words in numbers 6–11, omit the nonsense words from the boxes.

6   Can you read the words in the box?

7   Can you read the words in the box?

8   Can you read the words in the box?

9   Can you read the words in the box?

10   Can you read the words in the box?

11   Can you read the words in the box?

12   Can you read the row of words?

13   Can you read the row of words?

14   Can you read the box of words?

Directions for Scoring: Calculate the total number of correct responses for each skill and write it in the scoring table located at the end of the Teacher's Copy of the survey.

PHONICS SURVEY: TEACHER'S COPY

1   Letter Names of Capital Letters

P	W	T	X	Q	E	G	M	K
H	F	D	U	O	N	J	C	S
Z	Y	V	R	I	A	L	B	

2   Letter Names of Lowercase Letters

z	r	g	o	q	p	k	t	n
m	c	d	a	x	u	f	j	b
i	v	e						

3   Sounds of Vowels

a	o	e	i	u

4   Sounds of Consonants

d	l	t	n	h	v	g	k	r
p	w	y	z	c	x	b	s	m
c	f	j						

5   Diagraphs of Consonants

st	qu	ch	sh	th

6   Sounds of Short Vowels

log	pit	sat	nut	leg	(real)
sup	lem	git	gad	hoz	(nonsense)

7   Short Vowel with Consonant Diagraphs

lick	shop	chug	bench	thank	(real)
wuck	quan	thep	shig	chob	(nonsense)

8 Short Vowel with Consonant Blends

| crib | step | drum | glad | clog | (real) |
| trad | freg | drin | stom | pluf | (nonsense) |

9 Vowel + "e"

| rude | make | tile | note | seek | (real) |
| lote | gime | ruge | leep | fape | (nonsense) |

10 Diphthongs and Diagraphs with Vowels

moon	bull	should	moist	zoo
pout	bath	weather	lookout	boil
proud	owl	meant	dread	knock
boy	hound	lay	sigh	laid

11 R & L Controlled

| far | bolt | short | fall | clear | (real) |
| tirk | snarn | burl | larp | turst | (nonsense) |

12 Prefixes

| export | bicycle | unkind | subway | rewrite |

13 Suffixes

| smarter | lovely | watching | looked | beautiful |

14 Words with Multiple Syllables

| policeman | computer | invisible |
| principal | discovery | apologize |

SCORING

SKILL	SCORE	POSSIBLE SCORE	MASTERY
Letter Names of Capital Letters		26	
Letter Names of Lowercase Letters		21	
Sounds of Vowels		21	
Sounds of Consonants		5	
Diagraphs of Consonants		5	
DECODING			
Sounds of Short Vowel		10	
Short Vowel with Consonant Diagraphs		10	
Short Vowel with Consonant Blends		10	
Vowel + "e"		10	
Diphthongs and Diagraphs with Vowels		20	
R & L Controlled		10	
Prefixes		5	
Suffixes		5	
Words with Multiple Syllables		6	

PHONICS SURVEY: STUDENT COPY

1

P	W	T	X	Q	E	G	M	K
H	F	D	U	O	N	J	C	S
Z	Y	V	R	I	A	L	B	

2

z	r	g	o	q	p	k	t	n
m	c	d	a	x	u	f	j	b
i	v	e						

3

a		o		e		i		u

4

d	l	t	n	h	v	g	k	r
p	w	y	z	c	x	b	s	m
c	f	j						

ASSESSMENT EXAMPLE 2. PHONICS INVENTORY SAMPLE

5	st	qu	ch	sh	th	

6	log	pit	sat	nut	leg	(real)
	sup	lem	git	gad	hoz	(nonsense)

7	lick	shop	chug	bench	thank	(real)
	wuck	quan	thep	shig	chob	(nonsense)

8	crib	step	drum	glad	clog	(real)
	trad	freg	drin	stom	pluf	(nonsense)

9	rude	make	tile	note	seek	(real)
	lote	gime	ruge	leep	fape	(nonsense)

10	moon	bull	should	moist	zoo
	pout	bath	weather	lookout	boil
	proud	owl	meant	dread	knock
	boy	hound	lay	sigh	laid

11	far	bolt	short	fall	clear	(real)
	tirk	snarn	burl	larp	turst	(nonsense)

12	export	bicycle	unkind	subway	rewrite

13	smarter	lovely	watching	looked	beautiful

14	policeman	computer	invisible
	principal	discovery	apologize

SUMMARY OF PHONICS SKILLS

SKILL	DATE	SCORE	DATE	SCORE	DATE	SCORE	DATE MASTERED
Letter Names of Capital Letters							
Letter Names of Lowercase Letters							
Sounds of Vowels							
Sounds of Consonants							
Diagraphs of Consonants							
Sounds of Short Vowel							
Short Vowel with Consonant Diagraphs							
Short Vowel with Consonant Blends							
Vowel + "e"							
Diphthongs and Diagraphs with Vowels							
R & L Controlled							
Prefixes							
Suffixes							
Words with Multiple Syllables							

Interactive Assessment Work-Map

1
START HERE

Directions

For the example assessment above you are now going to "interact" with it as you check off criteria and write brief statements and definitions about its general type and, specifically, its reliability, validity, value and utility technical characteristics. You are encouraged to infer how the assessment might be used in your own teaching if applicable.

2
How Is the Assessment Administered?

Individual ☐

Group ☐

3

Note that an assessment can contain multiple types and/or degrees of type.

Assessment, Test, Measurement, Evaluation Type

Test ☐ Achievement in what academic area/subject/domain? _____

Quiz ☐ For reinforcement/application or demonstrated understanding _____

Survey ☐ Cognitive and/or behavioral

Portfolio ☐ Collection of artifacts for learner demonstration of meeting various criteria and/or understanding

Inventory ☐ Collection of items/prompts for discernment of learning in a comprehensive manner, with all sub-elements of that area included _____

Artifact ☐ Specific evidence to learner demonstration of among various criteria and/or understanding

Exam ☐ Measuring specific content-area aligned to specific learning objectives

Case ☐ A specific unit of analysis or person with defined boundaries

Writing Prompt ☐ A query, question or directive to guide student writing

Content Area Performance/Presentation ☐

4

Reliability and Validity

Reliable ☐
- - - - - - - - - - - -
Valid **FOR WHAT PURPOSE?**
Describe assessment features that support the validity type/s identification.

-Face ☐

-Content ☐

-Criterion-related ☐

-Construct ☐

-Concurrent ☐

-Predictive ☐

-Developmental ☐

5

Qualities and Characteristics

Check each box that applies and briefly notate how the assessment meets these defined criteria for assessment purpose, making inferences from results and interpreting data.

☐ Static- _____ Dynamic ☐

☐ Developmental

☐ Vertical

☐ Formative _____ Summative ☐

☐ Value for Who/When/How?

-Student ☐
-Teacher ☐
-Parent ☐
-Administrator ☐
-Community ☐

Utility ☐ (Leading to specific Actions) _____

Interactive Assessment Work-Map developed by M. Mott (2016).

Interactive Assessment Work-Map NOTES

Reliability and Validity Description

6

Reliable ☐

Valid **_FOR WHAT PURPOSE?_** *Describe assessment features that support the validity type/s identification. See information on validity definitions in the Reliability, Validity, Value, and Utility section of this book.*

-Face ☐

-Content ☐

-Criterion-related ☐

-Construct ☐

-Concurrent ☐

-Predictive ☐

-Developmental ☐

Interactive Assessment Work-Map developed by M. Mott (2016).

Interactive Assessment Work-Map NOTES

Value and Utility

Discuss and describe the educational value of the assessment under review. What does it do? Who does it help and how? Why can it inform teaching and learning? Can it inform educational policy and leadership decision making? In what manner?

7

Value for …?

Students ☐
- Content Area
- Cognitive
- Social-Emotional

-Teachers ☐
- Inform Instruction
- Formative
- Summative
- Dynamic

Utility for …?

-Administrators ☐
- Support Supervision Goals and Policy
- Guide Schoolwide Efforts and Programming

-Parents and Community ☐
- Information for Parents on Status of Education

Interactive Assessment Work-Map developed by M. Mott (2016).

Interactive Assessment Work-Map NOTES

Applications to *Your Professional Practice*

8

Given the reliability, validity, value, and utility characteristics of the current assessment under review, discuss and describe how you would apply it in your professional practice. Hypothetically illustrate a reasoned use for the assessment and freely identify its strengths and limitations (validity issues) for making inferences from the results of the assessment for instruction.

Interactive Assessment Work-Map developed by M. Mott (2016).

ASSESSMENT EXAMPLE 3. DEVELOPMENTAL SPELLING INVENTORY SAMPLE

BRIEF SAMPLE OF A DEVELOPMENTAL SPELLING ASSESSMENT[1]

DEVELOPMENT OF ORTHOGRAPHIC KNOWLEDGE

Many years ago, Kathy Ganske (1999) defined spelling and writing through the lens of language and symbolic interpretation and identified the developmental nature of the orthographic language system. Since then, we now have "developmental spelling" in myriad form utilized in K–6. Orthography is a linguistic-cognitive (or psycholinguistic) system that involves how we make sense of symbols, or letters and clumps of letters, in an increasingly sophisticated manner via instruction and experience as we grow. Since her work and that of others (Bear 2009), we continue to view the teaching of spelling and writing from a developmental perspective. Writing and spelling ability is thus developmental and takes

---

1   The current section is based upon Ganske's (1999) work addressing orthographic development.

place in stages. Slowly disappearing (not fast enough!) is the old "spelling test" that a student memorizes and then takes on a Friday. One might hypothesize that this measure is valid for making inferences about the degree to which the students' parents are diligent or not in encouraging the child to do his memorization study.

Rather than looking at a spelling list, Developmental Spelling Assessment (DSA) seeks to determine a student's level of understanding of how words are constructed and, for younger children, how letters relate to corresponding sounds. Children develop an increasingly sophisticated understanding of the structure of words. The DSA enables teachers to level each student to focus instruction on the word structure patterns that student needs to learn to move up to the next level. Examples of spelling developmental levels (scope and sequence) are:

1   Letter Name (moving then from consonants to vowels and vowel teams).

2   Consonant-Vowel-Consonant (CVC) words such as bat; hat; mat; cat.

3   Advanced vowel generalizations such as ough for the /O/ sound or igh for the /I/ sound.

4   Within word structures such as words with multiple morphemes (lovingly) to multisyllabic words such as lament; bending; shatter; and disengage.

5   Advanced words with a clear etymological basis such as biology; philology; disinclined; disrobe; disrespect.

TEACHER PROMPT FOR EARLY ELEMENTARY SPELLING WORDS

Directions:

1   Tell the students that you are going to give them words to spell so that you can teach them more effectively by learning how they spell.

2   Read each word.

3   Follow with the word in the sentence.

4   State the word one last time.

5   Proceed and do the same for all twenty words.

6   Analyze the results (see Analysis directions).

7   Teach phonics, word structure and identification to individuals and small groups of students.

SAMPLE SPELLING WORD LIST

1   No. "No," he told his brother. No

2   Bat. The girl hit the ball with the bat. Bat

3   Crate. He put the supplies in the crate. Crate

4   Sift. He had to sift the flour. Sift

5   Patch. He placed a patch on the hole. Patch

6   Tree. The tree had no leaves in the winter. Tree

7   Square. A square has four sides. Square

8   Time. He knew it was time to leave. Time

9   Leader. The leader led the group. Leader

10   Moon. There is a full moon tonight. Moon

11   Coin. He had one coin and one dollar bill. Coin

12   Bent. The metal frame was bent. Bent

13   Brisk. She walked at a brisk pace. Brisk

14   Ketchup. He put ketchup on the fries. Ketchup

15   Chef. The chef prepared the dinner. Chef

16   Monster. The monster was not scary at all. Monster

17   Bait. The fish bit the hook with the bait. Bait

18   Lightning. The storm brought lightning. Lightning

19   Inertia. The inertia of the earthquake caused the ground to move. Inertia

20   Restaurant. We ate a great dinner at the restaurant. Restaurant

TYPICAL SPELLING PROGRESSION AND ERRORS

The chart below provides a developmental snapshot of spellings by children as they react to the spelling assessment conducted by the teacher. Based upon their spellings, the teacher will analyze (see next section) constructed words to then identify what type of phonics or word structure to teach.

		Letter Name	CVC		Within Word	Advanced		
1.	No.	n;		no				
2.	Bat.	b; bt;		bat				
3.	Crate	krt; krat;	krate;		crait		crate	
4.	Sift	sf; sft		sif		sift		
5.	Patch	p; pc		pat		pach		patch
6.	Tree	t; tr;		tre		tree		
7.	Square	sr; skr		sqr		sqar		square
8.	Time	t; tm		tim		time		

#	Word				
9.	Leader	ldr	ledr	leder	leader
10.	Moon	m; mn	mun	moon	
11.	Coin	k; kn	con	cone	coin
12.	Bent	b; bn	bnt	ben	bent
13.	Brisk	brk	brsk	brik	brisk
14.	Ketchup	k; kp	kejp	kejup	kecthup
15.	Chef	s; sf	shf	shef	chef
16.	Monster	m; msr	mnstr	monster	
17.	Bait	b; bt	bat	bate	bait
18.	Lightning	l; lt	litn	litning	lightning
19.	Inertia	n	inrsh	inersha	inertia
20.	Restaurant	r; rs	resternt	resteront	restaurant

ANALYZING RESULTS
GENERATING SPECIFIC INSTRUCTIONAL OBJECTIVES OF SPELLING/WORD STRUCTURE FOR INDIVIDUAL STUDENTS

After conducting the whole-group administered developmental spelling assessment, you will analyze individual student spellings to discern their knowledge of the orthographic system of letters representing sounds, aligned symbol-letters, and words. When a word is misspelled, you can circle the type of misspelling they represented on the error guide above, thus giving you a graphical look at what column most of their spellings fall under. Using the chart of sample spellings above, you can identify their spelling patterns, or developmental level of phonics/word study, by seeing what kinds of errors they generate. For example, if a student spells "bat" as bt, they are in the "Letter Name" developmental spelling level and the teacher would then teach long and short vowels. Likewise, if a more advanced student spells "restaurant" as "resteront," they need to be taught advanced word complexity such as etymology of word spellings. In the case of "restaurant," the instructional objective for that speller would center on the French derivational spellings, including the "au" and "ant" endings and maybe the advanced vowel generalizations included in French-derived words such as "boutique," etc.

Interactive Assessment Work-Map

Directions

For the example assessment above you are now going to "interact" with it as you check off criteria and write brief statements and definitions about its general type and, specifically, its reliability, validity, value and utility technical characteristics. You are encouraged to infer how the assessment might be used in your own teaching if applicable.

START HERE

1

How Is the Assessment Administered?

2

Individual ☐

Group ☐

3

Assessment, Test, Measurement, Evaluation Type

Note that an assessment can contain multiple types and/or degrees of type.

Test ☐ Achievement in what academic area/subject/domain? _____

Quiz ☐ For reinforcement/application or demonstrated understanding _____

Survey ☐ Cognitive and/or behavioral _____

Portfolio ☐ Collection of artifacts for learner demonstration of meeting various criteria and/or understanding

Inventory ☐ Collection of items/prompts for discernment of learning in a comprehensive manner, with all sub-elements of that area included _____

Artifact ☐ Specific evidence to learner demonstration of among various criteria and/or understanding

Exam ☐ Measuring specific content-area aligned to specific learning objectives _____

Case ☐ A specific unit of analysis or person with defined boundaries _____

Writing Prompt ☐ A query, question or directive to guide student writing _____

Content Area Performance/Presentation ☐ _____

Qualities and Characteristics

Check each box that applies and briefly notate how the assessment meets these defined criteria for assessment purpose, making inferences from results and interpreting data.

☐ Static- _____ Dynamic ☐

☐ Developmental

☐ Vertical

☐ Formative _____ Summative ☐

☐ Value for Who/When/How?

-Student ☐
-Teacher ☐
-Parent ☐
-Administrator ☐
-Community ☐

Utility ☐ (Leading to specific Actions) _____

5

Reliability and Validity

Reliable ☐

Valid *FOR WHAT PURPOSE?*
Describe assessment features that support the validity type/s identification.

-Face ☐

-Content ☐

-Criterion-related ☐

-Construct ☐

-Concurrent ☐

-Predictive ☐

-Developmental ☐

4

Interactive Assessment Work-Map developed by M. Mott (2016).

Interactive Assessment Work-Map NOTES

6

Reliability and Validity Description

Reliable ☐

Valid **_FOR WHAT PURPOSE?_** *Describe assessment features that support the validity type/s identification. See information on validity definitions in the Reliability, Validity, Value, and Utility section of this book.*

-Face ☐

-Content ☐

-Criterion-related ☐

-Construct ☐

-Concurrent ☐

-Predictive ☐

-Developmental ☐

Interactive Assessment Work-Map developed by M. Mott (2016).

Interactive Assessment Work-Map NOTES

Value and Utility

Discuss and describe the educational value of the assessment under review. What does it do? Who does it help and how? Why can it inform teaching and learning? Can it inform educational policy and leadership decision making? In what manner?

7

Value for ...?

Students ☐
-Content Area
-Cognitive
-Social-Emotional
-Teachers ☐
-Inform Instruction
-Formative
-Summative
-Dynamic
Utility for ...?
-Administrators ☐
-Support Supervision Goals and Policy
-Guide Schoolwide Efforts and Programming
-Parents and Community ☐
-Information for Parents on Status of Education

Interactive Assessment Work-Map developed by M. Mott (2016).

Interactive Assessment Work-Map NOTES

Applications to *Your Professional Practice*

8

Given the reliability, validity, value, and utility characteristics of the current assessment under review, discuss and describe how you would apply it in your professional practice. Hypothetically illustrate a reasoned use for the assessment and freely identify its strengths and limitations (validity issues) for making inferences from the results of the assessment for instruction.

Interactive Assessment Work-Map developed by M. Mott (2016).

ASSESSMENT EXAMPLE 4. NARRATIVE WRITING RUBRIC FOR MEDIA (WWYR)

The following assessment example is extracted from the *Early Childhood Research and Practice* journal article "Applying an Analytic Writing Rubric to Children's Hypermedia 'Narratives,'" by Michael Seth Mott, Cynthia Etsler, and Deondra Drumgold.

RESEARCH AND SAMPLE RUBRIC

In an effort designed to guide and improve the assessment of a newly developed writing environment, the reliability and developmental and concurrent validity of a previously validated rubric developed for pen-and-paper-created narratives, Writing What You Read (WWYR), was determined when applied to hypermedia-authored narratives of children in second and third grades. Children (n = 60) from four intact classrooms produced hypermedia narratives (text, audio, graphic, and video elements) over a four-month period in a school-based computer laboratory. Raters (n = 5) with knowledge of the teaching of process writing and use of hypermedia software judged the hypermedia narrative productions. Raters judged all students' (n = 60) hypermedia narrative productions individually without resolving differences through discussion. Two analyses were used to determine reliability: percentages of agreement and Pearson correlations. Percentages of agreement for the WWYR rubric averaged across ten pairs of raters found high percentages of agreement among raters (.70 for ±0 and .99 for ±1). Pearson correlations averaged across ten pairs of raters found acceptable interrater reliability for four of the five subscales. For the five subscales (Theme, Character, Setting, Plot, and Communication), the r values were .59, .55, .49, .50, and .50, respectively. Developmental validity of the WWYR scores was examined with one-way MANOVA to evaluate the WWYR scores of children grouped as low, medium, or high ability based on their Iowa Test of Basic Skills (ITBS) National Percentile Rank for Literacy Skill. Evidence for the developmental validity of the WWYR scores was supported across the three ability groups, $F(2, 36) = 2.59$, $p < .01$. Concurrent validity was examined through correlational analysis between students' mean WWYR score and ITBS score. Scores from the two measures were positively correlated, $r = .83$, $p < .01$, providing evidence of the sensitivity of the WWYR assessment to measure the developmental literacy competency of the third-grade students. Results support teachers' use of a validated rubric developed for pen-and-paper-created narratives applied to hypermedia narratives, despite additional visual and audio narrative elements inherent to hypermedia. Implications for literacy teaching and learning with hypermedia address core questions about the similarities and differences between written textual expression and visual and verbally recorded expression. A revised and expanded WWYR rubric is proposed to begin to address these core questions generated by teachers' use of the hypermedia writing environment.

INTRODUCTION

The very notion of "writing" is increasingly being transformed by new digital computer technologies in society, homes, businesses, and schools. Today, one's ability to represent thought electronically is more important than ever. The extreme pace of change in society dictates that early childhood educators consider how to facilitate children in learning to express themselves digitally in computer environments in developmentally appropriate ways. This article addresses the curriculum, instruction, and assessment of children's written expression in hypermedia, a computer environment that supports text, audio, video, and graphics. The hypermedia curriculum and instruction are described, and a technical analysis of a proposed assessment is applied and discussed.

EMERGING TRENDS

Prior research has addressed the reliability and validity of a narrative rubric useful for both teaching and learning (value) and large-scale (utility) literacy assessment. As literacy curriculum and instruction continue to transform to include new computer-based learning environments, researchers must correspondingly develop and technically evaluate assessments for the new environments. Hypermedia represents a powerful electronic environment through which literacy expression can be facilitated by the manipulation of text, graphics, audio, and video elements, and this technology and integration are reflected in the new literacy K–12 standards (IRA and NCTE 2001). The qualities of hypermedia that support higher-level cognitive processes such as synthesis, organization, evaluation, and reflexivity have been well documented (Yang 1996; Mott, Sumrall, and Hodges 1997). However, there is a glaring absence of ways to reliably and validly assess students' hypermedia products. To address this absence, a narrative process writing curriculum and instruction environment was merged with hypermedia. These terms are defined as follows:

- Process writing curriculum and instruction: writing using discrete stages (brainstorming, drafting, conferencing, revising, editing, and publishing) administered via "minilessons" applied to address the needs of the individual writers in whole-group instruction. See Graves (1983) for a detailed description.
- Hypermedia: Hypermedia comprises two main components: (1) hyper: the ability to program electronic links, or hyperconnections, to connect information to any other Internet-based source or simply to link locally to a hard drive or diskette, and (2) media: the ability to manipulate multiple meaning-based symbol systems representing a variety of sources—text, graphics, audio, and video clips.

This article addresses the reliability and developmental and concurrent validity of a previously validated narrative writing rubric, Writing What You Read (WWYR) (Wolf and Gearhart 1994; Novak, Herman, and Gearhart 1996), applied to hypermedia narratives created by students in grades 2 and 3 (see Table 4.1). The technical qualities of the process-oriented classroom rubric, valuable for teaching and learning on a day-to-day basis, are linked to the utility of the narrative rubric for measuring elementary students' literacy competencies as identified via a validated large-scale instrument, the Iowa Test of Basic Skills—Literacy Competency. Thus, five main issues are addressed relating to rater judgments of elementary students' hypermedia narratives (stories with text, graphics, audio, and video elements authored using HyperStudio hypermedia software):

- Reliability of interrater judgments is examined using the WWYR of hypermedia narrative quality.
- Developmental validity of the WWYR scores is examined with one-way MANOVA used to evaluate the WWYR scores of students grouped as low, medium, or high ability based on their Iowa Test of Basic Skills (ITBS) National Percentile Rank for Literacy Skill.
- Concurrent validity is examined through correlational analysis of students' mean WWYR scores and ITBS scores.
- Value of the WWYR for use as a teaching tool is summarized through reviewing the genesis of the rubric as demonstrated in its path from creation for pen-and-paper narratives to hypermedia narratives as evaluated in multiple studies.
- Utility of the WWYR applied to students' hypermedia narratives is addressed to reveal possible alignment between the innovative curriculum and instruction addressed in the current study with ITBS- and WWYR-identified literacy levels.

RESEARCH COMPONENTS

METHODS

Children (n = 60) from four intact classrooms (two second-grade and two third-grade classrooms) produced hypermedia narratives over a four-month period in a school-based computer laboratory equipped with ten Windows-based microcomputers. Raters/(Teachers) (n = 5) with knowledge of the teaching of process writing and use of hypermedia software judged the hypermedia narrative productions. An interactive hypermedia software tutorial program was developed and used to train the teachers (n = 4) in the implementation of process writing techniques in conjunction with the use of hypermedia features as part of their elementary curriculum. Raters participated in a three-hour training-and-rating session in a university computer laboratory equipped with five Power Macintosh microcomputers. Raters judged all students' (n = 60) hypermedia narrative productions individually without resolving differences through discussion.

MATERIALS

The WWYR rubric shown in Table 4.1 contained five evaluative scales designed to assess students' developing competencies in narrative writing: Theme, Character, Setting, Plot, and Communication. The vertical analytical evaluative scales (1–6 for each competency) were designed to enable teachers to make instructional decisions on specific narrative components

Table 4.1 Writing What You Read Narrative Rubric (Wolf and Gearhart 1994)

THEME	CHARACTER	SETTING	PLOT	COMMUNICATION
Explicit–Implicit	Flat–Round	Backdrop–Essential	Simple–Complex	Context-bound
Didactic–Revealing	Static–Dynamic	Simple–Multifunctional	Static–Conflict	Literal–Symbolic
1: Not present or not developed through other narrative elements	1: One or two flat, static characters, with little relationship between characters	1: Backdrop setting with little or no indication of time or place ("There was a little girl. She liked candy.")	1: One or two events with little or no conflict ("Once there was a cat. The cat liked milk.")	1: Writing bound to context (you have to be there) and often dependent on drawing and talk to clarify the meaning
2: Meaning centered in a series of list-like statements ("I like my mom. And I like my dad. And I like my …")	2: Some rounding, usually in physical description; relationship between characters is action driven	2: Skeletal indication of time and place often held in past time ("Once there was …"); little relationship to other narrative elements	2: Beginning sequence of events but out-of-sync occurrences; events without problem; problem without resolution	2: Beginning awareness of reader consider-ations; straightforward style and tone focused on getting the information out
3: Beginning statement of theme, often explicit and didactic ("The mean witch chased the children, and she shouldn't have done that.")	3: Continued rounding in physical description, particularly stereotyp-ical features ("wart on the end of her nose")	3: Beginning relation-ship between setting and other narrative elements (futuristic setting to accommodate aliens and spaceships)	3: Single linear episode with clear beginning, middle, and end; the episode contains a problem, emotional response, action, and outcome	3: Writer begins to make sense of explanations and transitions ("because" and "so"); literal style centers on description
4: Beginning revelation of theme on both explicit and implicit levels through the more subtle things characters say and do	4: Beginning insights into motivation and intention that drive the feeling and action of main characters, often through limited omniscient point of view	4: Setting becomes more essential to the development of the story in explicit ways: characters may remark on the setting, or the time and place may be integral to the plot	4: Plot increases in complexity with more than one episode; each episode contains problem, emotional response, action, and outcome	4: Increased information and explanation for the reader (linking ideas as well as episodes); words more carefully selected to suit the narrative's purpose
5: Beginning use of secondary themes, often tied to overarching theme but sometimes tangential	5: Further rounding (in feeling and motivation); dynamic features appear in central characters and between characters	5: Setting may serve more than one function, and the relationship between functions is more implicit and symbolic	5: Stronger relationships between episodes (with resolution in one leading to a problem in the next)	5: Some experimen-tation with symbolism (particularly figurative language), which shows reader considerations
6: Overarching theme multilayered and complex; secondary themes integrally related to the primary themes	6: Round, dynamic major characters through rich description of affect, intention, and motivation	6: Setting fully integrated with the characters, action, and theme	6: Overarching problem and resolution supported by multiple episodes	6: Careful crafting of choices of story structure as well as vocabulary demonstrate considerate orchestra-tion of all resources

needing reinforcement and were not intended as a method for assigning a numerical value to a narrative. Teachers merely had to shade a box in the rubric to denote where a child's narrative was along each competency. The ITBS (Linn and Wilson 1990) Form J was used as a basic battery for grades K–9 and included language skills directly related to writing: word analysis, vocabulary, spelling, and reading comprehension. Reliability coefficients for Form J ranged from .70–.90 for the language skills components. Additionally, the ITBS met high standards of overall technical quality and has been a widely accepted standardized measure of cognitive skill.

HYPERMEDIA NARRATIVES

HyperStudio Presentation Software (Wagner 1997–2001) was used to support the children in expressing themselves with text, audio, video, and graphic elements in their narrative productions (see Figures 4.1–4.4). Children composed on paper and computer, with teachers structuring the process with Writing Workshop (Graves 1983), a method for organizing writing into discrete and recursive stages. These stages are (1) brainstorming, (2) revising,

Figure 4.1

HyperStudio narrative "page" with hypermedia elements: Grade 2.

(3) drafting, (4) peer conferencing, (5) editing, and (6) publishing (see Mott and Klomes 2001 for a detailed description of a program similar to the program addressed in the current study).

Elements shown are (1) graphics text, (2) paint bucket tool (blue), (3) line tool: freehand, and (4) hyperconnection or link to "Page 1" via button.

HyperStudio was selected for this project for a number of reasons: (1) it supports high-end features such as video and animation; (2) it is relatively easy to use, even by young children (grades 1–3); (3) it contains a flexible interface; and (4) it is the most widely used multimedia/hypermedia platform in elementary education, with over one hundred thousand users (Wagner 1997–2001). HyperStudio contains several programming features that support children's hypermedia programming (see Figures 4.5–4.10). Programming instruction (and writing workshops) occurred through minilessons over a four-month period. Figures 4.5 through 4.10 contain examples from a minilesson.

The line tool was introduced to children during their first programming minilessons.

The "hyper" programming tool, button creation, enabled children to connect cards (narrative pages) to other cards. Button creation supported linear links (card 1 to 2 to 3), suitable for early childhood.

Figure 4.2

Page with the following features: textbox/word-processed text with scrolling and a graphic (cat) inserted into Shape.

Figure 4.3

HyperStudio page. Note control of font, color, background color, and font size.

Figure 4.4

This page includes a scanned photograph.

Figure 4.5

This page contains the programming line tool.

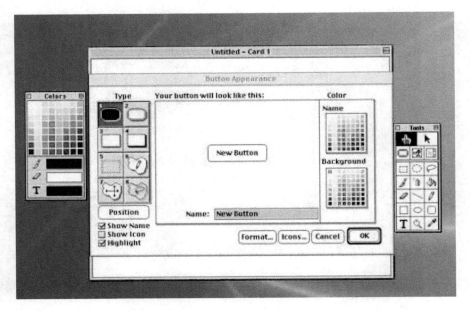

Figure 4.6

This page contains the hyperconnection programming tool.

ASSESSMENT EXAMPLE 4. NARRATIVE WRITING RUBRIC FOR MEDIA (WWYR)

Figure 4.7

This page contains the graphics tool. Children inserted graphics and scanned images from art representing many media: watercolor, acrylic paint, crayons, and colored pencils.

Figure 4.8

This page contains the textbox tool (word processing).

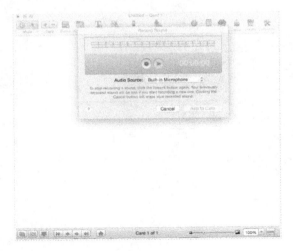

Figure 4.9

This page contains the digital audio deck.

Figure 4.10

This page contains video control.

Table 4.2 Percentages of Agreement for all Five Subscales of the WWYR Rubric

WWYR SUBSCALE	±0	±1	N
Theme	.70	.96	60
Character	.78	.99	60
Plot	.73	.99	60
Setting	.67	.99	60
Communication	.68	.99	60

Writing was accomplished via the textbox tool that functions as a word processor with editing tools, cutting, pasting, and other word processor capabilities.

Children inserted audio clips, programmed via button creation, to enrich their text. Audio clips were recorded by the author or downloaded from HyperStudio for special effects such as an alarm clock sound.

Video clips were inserted, programmed via button creation, to supplement the narrative. One example was a video clip of Mars used in a science fiction narrative by a third-grade student.

RELIABILITY

PERCENTAGES OF AGREEMENT

Percentages of agreement for the WWYR rubric averaged across ten pairs of raters found high percentages of agreement among raters (.70 for ±0 and .99 for ±1) (see Table 4.2). The ±0 and ±1 percentages of agreement across ten pairs of raters were higher than the ±0 and ±1 agreement levels found in both the Gearhart, Herman, Novack, and Wolf (1995) and Novak, Herman, and Gearhart (1996) WWYR reliability studies (compared in Table 4.3). The high percentages of agreement found in this study may be attributed to the raters' use of only

Table 4.3 Percentages of Agreement for the WWYR Rubric Averaged across All Subscales

WWYR RATING MATERIAL AND GRADE	±0	±1	n
Hypermedia Narratives: Grades 2–3 Mott & Sumrall (1998)	.71	.98	60
Pen-and-Paper Narratives: Grades 1–6 Gearhart, Herman, Novak, and Wolf (1995)	.46	.96	120
Collections of Pen-and-Paper Narratives: Grades 2–5 Novak, Herman, and Gearhart (1996)	.25	.94	52

Table 4.4 Average Pearson Correlations for WWYR Rubric Scoring across Ten Pairs of Raters

WWYR RATING MATERIAL AND GRADE		THEME	CHARACTER	SETTING	PLOT	COMMUNICATION
Hypermedia Narratives: Grades 2–3	r	.59	.55	.49	.50	.50
Mott & Sumrall 1998 (n = 60)	SD	.25	.31	.25	.29	.24
Pen-and-Paper Narratives Grades 1–6	r	.64	.59	.48	.57	.66
Gearhart et al. (1995) (n = 120)	SD	.10	.10	.12	.14	.10

the first three WWYR rubric evaluative subscale levels. The WWYR rubric contains six subscale levels that are developmentally sequenced according to the varied writing competencies of students in grades K–6. Because students in this study were in second and third grade, raters typically applied only levels 1, 2, and 3 out of five total levels. This narrow range of values independently applied by raters limited the number of choices. Hence, high percentages of agreement between raters would be expected based on the limited number of scale levels used.

The percentages of agreement that were revealed in the current study, although higher than those found in the Gearhart, Herman, Novak, and Wolf (1995) study, should be considered descriptive information. Gearhart et al. remarked that percentages of agreement found for the WWYR should not be interpreted as "strong evidence of reliability" (p. 224). Rather, percentages of agreement can be used to help identify the existence of widely varying patterns of rater judgments, both across WWYR subscales and across all rater pairs. No such widely varying patterns were found in the current study. The limitations of analyses involving percentages of agreement analysis were discussed by Abedi (1994), who argued that, although percentages of agreement can reveal the existence of widely varying patterns of agreement among raters, they can also yield different results from other analyses such as Pearson correlations.

PEARSON CORRELATIONS

Pearson correlations were used to further examine reliability of rater judgments. Pearson correlations averaged across ten pairs of raters found acceptable interrater reliability for four of the five subscales. For the five subscales (Theme, Character, Setting, Plot, and Communication), the r values were .59, .55, .49, .50 and .50. Table 4.4 contains the results of the Pearson correlations for WWYR rubric scoring across all rater pairs for the current study and for the Gearhart et al. (1995) study. An examination of correlation scores for hypermedia narrative productions revealed that interrater reliability for four of the five WWYR subscales (Theme,

ASSESSMENT EXAMPLE 4. NARRATIVE WRITING RUBRIC FOR MEDIA (WWYR)

Table 4.5 Comparison of WWYR Subscale Correlations: Pen-and-Paper Narratives versus Hypermedia

SUBSCALE	THEME	CHARACTER	SETTING	PLOT	COMMUNICATION
SAMPLES (N = 60) MOTT AND SUMRALL (1998) HYPERMEDIA					
Theme	--	.86*	.79*	.79*	.73*
Character	--	--	.74*	.74*	.76*
Setting	--	--	--	.75*	.68*
Plot	--	--	--	--	.78*
Communication	--	--	--	--	--
SAMPLES (N = 120) GEARHART ET AL. (1995) PEN-AND-PAPER NARRATIVES					
Theme	--	.83*	.81*	.83*	.86*
Character	--	--	.82*	.87*	.86*
Setting	--	--	--	.73*	.86*
Plot	--	--	--	--	.85*
Communication	--	--	--	--	--

Note: *p < .001.

Character, Setting, and Plot) was comparable to the interrater reliability levels found in the Gearhart et al. (1995) WWYR reliability study for pen-and-paper-created narratives. For the fifth subscale (Communication), however, the correlational coefficient value was .16 higher in the Gearhart et al. study than in the current study. Despite the lower value found in the current study for Communication, Gearhart et al. related that an average subscale correlation higher than .50 could be considered adequate for a rubric such as the WWYR. Table 4.5 summarizes the comparison of WWYR correlations across all subscales for the current study and those found in the literature (Gearhart et al. 1995; Novak et al. 1996).

The WWYR correlations observed in this study as well as in the Gearhart et al. (1995) study demonstrated that ratings were highly correlated across all subscales. The r values were low in this study as well as in the Gearhart et al. (1995) and Novak et al. (1996) studies. However, set guidelines for what is an acceptable level of interrater reliability do not exist. Nonetheless, both Gearhart et al. and Novak et al., whose studies analyzed holistic scores derived from the combined r values of Theme, Character, Plot, Setting, and Communication, argued that r values that fell within the .50 to .70 range were acceptable for analytic writing rubrics. In the current study, the interrater reliability for Theme, Character, Plot, and Communication subscales fell within the .50 and .59 range, but the level of interrater reliability (r = .49) for the Setting subscale did not. It is important to note that, in the Gearhart et al. (1995) study, a low coefficient value for the subscale of Setting was also found (r = .48). The acceptable interrater reliabilities for Theme, Character, Plot, and Communication in this study were comparable to the acceptable levels found in the Gearhart et al. (1995) study, and the r values for the Setting subscale in both this study and the Gearhart et al. (1995) study were not acceptable (albeit by large-scale standards). It is important to note that interrater reliability levels for Theme, Character, and Plot in this study may have been lower than the r values in the Gearhart et al. (1995) study because the researcher applied more stringent rating procedures in this study. Raters in the Gearhart et al. (1995) study were permitted to resolve differences greater than one scale point through discussion, whereas raters in this study were not permitted to resolve differences. In the current study, all ratings were included in the final data set.

The highly correlated rater judgments, along all five WWYR subscales for the current study and for the Gearhart et al. (1995) study, provided further evidence of the reliability of WWYR raters' judgments. The true function of a writing rubric is that it "enables raters to apply standard criteria in making judgments about the quality of students' work" (Abedi 1994, p. 8). Gearhart et al. (1995), Novak et al. (1996), and Abedi (1994) argued that highly correlated scores across rubric subscales can be viewed as a positive indication that raters' judgments are being consistently applied.

Table 4.6 Descriptive Statistics: WWYR Subscales across ITBS Ability Level

STATISTICS	DEPENDENT VARIABLES					
	n	THEME	CHARACTER	SETTING	PLOT	COMMUNICATION
Mean Vectors						
ITBS ABILITY LEVEL						
Low	13	2.31	1.80	1.96	2.10	2.14
Medium	13	2.80	2.34	2.32	2.66	2.52
High	14	2.86	2.60	2.66	2.74	2.77
VARIANCE–COVARIANCE MATRIX						
Theme		.21	.15	.19	.13	.11
Character		--	.23	.13	.15	.13
Setting		--	--	.19	.14	.11
Plot		--	--	--	.19	.14
Communication		--	--	--	--	.16

Table 4.7 Mean WWYR Subscale Scores for Low-, Medium-, and High-Ability Grade-3 Students

WWYR SUBSCALE	ITBS NPR/ LITERACY CATEGORY	MEAN SCORE	SD	n	F	Sig
Theme	Low	2.31	.62	16		
	Medium	2.80	.28	10	6.19	.01
	High	2.86	.31	13		
Character	Low	1.80	.50	16		
	Medium	2.34	.38	10	10.77	.01
	High	2.60	.51	13		
Setting	Low	1.96	.42	16		
	Medium	2.32	.56	19	9.34	.01
	High	2.66	.34	13		
Plot	Low	2.10	.54	16		
	Medium	2.66	.34	10	9.28	.01
	High	2.74	.34	13		
Communication	Low	2.14	.47	16		
	Medium	2.52	.34	10	9.20	.01
	High	2.77	.35	13		

VALIDITY

DEVELOPMENTAL VALIDITY

Developmental validity of WWYR scores was examined via one-way MANOVA conducted on the low-, medium-, and high-ability vectors of WWYR subscale scores. The assumption for this analysis was based upon the technical qualities of the ITBS—Literacy measure to delineate the developmental literacy levels of the children. Results indicated a statistically significant difference between the three ability groups ($F(2, 36) = 2.59$, $p = .01$). Table 4.6 provides descriptive statistics, and Table 4.7 provides an additional summary of these results across each of the five WWYR subscales.

Tukey HSD tests were conducted on the mean vector scores of the three ability groups for all five WWYR subscales to follow up these results. For the WWYR subscale of Theme, low-ability students (M = 2.31, SD = .62) received lower scores than both medium-ability students (M = 2.80, SD = .28) and high-ability students (M = 2.86, SD = .31). For the WWYR subscales of Character, Setting, Plot, and Communication, all differences were significant. Therefore, low-ability students' scores were significantly lower than medium-ability students' scores, which were significantly lower than the high-ability students' scores. The significant differences revealed between low, medium, and high ITBS groups and the WWYR subscale

Table 4.8 Frequency of HyperStudio Multimedia Features Used in Students' Hypermedia Narrative Productions*

GRADE LEVEL	BUTTON WITH HYPERMEDIA LINK	BUTTON WITH AUDIO	BUTTON WITH VIDEO	TEXT BOX	GRAPHICS TEXT	SCANNED ART	GRAPHICS OBJECTS (CLIP ART)
2 (n = 20)	100%	81%	0%	100%	45%	96%	82%
3 (n = 40)	100%	100%	5%	100%	64%	100%	100%

*Note. In three out of the four classrooms where hypermedia/writing occurred, students' use of hypermedia/multimedia features was controlled by the teachers.

scores provided evidence for the sensitivity of the WWYR to measure the development of students' hypermedia/writing competence. The significant results of the one-way MANOVA suggest that raters' judgments were evaluating students' skills as message producers (communication through text and other meaning-based symbol systems). The one-way MANOVA did not yield results that would enable the researcher to describe the degree of relatedness of raters' WWYR judgments and students' ITBS scores. In order to describe the relationship between WWYR scores and literacy skill (as measured by the ITBS), additional correlational analyses were conducted.

CONCURRENT VALIDITY

The observed Pearson r correlation revealed a positive relationship between students' average WWYR score (averaged across the subscales of Theme, Character, Setting, Plot, and Communication) and their ITBS National Percentile Rank (literacy skills score), $r = .83$, $p > .001$. The positive correlation ($r = .83$) between students' WWYR scores and ITBS scores revealed in this analysis provided evidence for the concurrent validity (the degree to which test scores are related to the scores on an already-established test) of WWYR raters' judgments of hypermedia productions. According to Messick (1992), establishment of the concurrent validity of a measure can be a stepping-stone toward establishment of the content-related validity (the degree to which scores evaluate the specific domain they were designed to evaluate) of a measure. Hence, the developmental and concurrent validities established for WWYR raters' judgments of hypermedia productions represented an important initial attempt toward eventually establishing the content-related validity of the WWYR when applied to hypermedia productions.

The strong positive linear relationship between ITBS literacy skill scores and WWYR rater judgments of hypermedia productions indicated that the hypermedia writing curriculum used in the current study involved literacy-based activities. The fact that students in this study expressed themselves through hypermedia features, and not solely through text, indicated that students' literacy skill can be enhanced through student expression via hypermedia and multimedia features. Table 4.8 provides additional information on the students' utilization of the hypermedia features used in their writing. This finding supported the claims of Daiute and Morse (1994), who observed that students who engaged in hypermedia writing developed literacy skill through the manipulation of text and other symbols. A weakness of the developmental and concurrent validity analyses was that evidence for obtaining the degree to which rater judgments of students' hypermedia productions evaluated textual features as well as textual and other hypermedia features (audio, hypermedia links, graphics, etc.) could not be determined.

ASSESSMENT VALUE AND UTILITY

The results of this study suggest several important implications for the assessment of students' hypermedia products. Having a reliable and valid assessment for evaluating students' hypermedia-based writing serves two general purposes: (1) to enhance classroom instruction

Table 4.9

HYPERMEDIA	THEME	CHARACTER	SETTING	PLOT	COMMUNICATION
Elements	Explicit–Implicit	Flat–Round	Backdrop–Essential	Simple–Complex	Context-bound
	Didactic–Revealing	Static–Dynamic	Simple–Multifunctional	Static–Conflict	Literal–Symbolic
-Text -Hypertext -Graphic -Audio -Video	1: Not present or not developed through other narrative elements	1: One or two flat, static characters, with little relationship between characters	1: Backdrop setting with little or no indication of time or place ("There was a little girl. She liked candy.")	1: One or two events with little or no conflict ("Once there was a cat. The cat liked milk.")	1: Writing bound to context (you have to be there) and often dependent on drawing and talk to clarify the meaning
-Text -Hypertext -Graphic -Audio -Video	2: Meaning centered in a series of list-like statements ("I like my mom. And I like my dad. And I like my …")	2: Some rounding, usually in physical description; relationship between characters is action driven	2: Skeletal indication of time and place often held in past time ("Once there was …"); little relationship to other narrative elements	2: Beginning sequence of events but out-of-sync occurrences; events without problem; problem without resolution	2: Beginning awareness of reader considerations; straightforward style and tone focused on getting the information out
-Text -Hypertext -Graphic -Audio -Video	3: Beginning statement of theme, often explicit and didactic ("The mean witch chased the children, and she shouldn't have done that.")	3: Continued rounding in physical description, particularly stereotypical features ("wart on the end of her nose")	3: Beginning relationship between setting and other narrative elements (futuristic setting to accommodate aliens and spaceships)	3: Single linear episode with clear beginning, middle, and end; the episode contains a problem, emotional response, action, and outcome	3: Writer begins to make sense of explanations and transitions ("because" and "so"); literal style centers on description

-Text -Hypertext -Graphic -Audio -Video	4: Beginning revelation of theme on both explicit and implicit levels through the more subtle things characters say and do	4: Beginning insights into motivation and intention that drive the feeling and action of main characters, often through limited omniscient point of view	4: Setting becomes more essential to the development of the story in explicit ways: characters may remark on the setting, or the time and place may be integral to the plot	4: Plot increases in complexity with more than one episode; each episode contains problem, emotional response, action, and outcome	4: Increased information and explanation for the reader (linking ideas as well as episodes); words more carefully selected to suit the narrative's purpose
-Text -Hypertext -Graphic -Audio -Video	5: Beginning use of secondary themes, often tied to overarching theme but sometimes tangential	5: Further rounding (in feeling and motivation); dynamic features appear in central characters and between characters	5: Setting may serve more than one function, and the relationship between functions is more implicit and symbolic	5: Stronger relationships between episodes (with resolution in one leading to a problem in the next)	5: Some experimentation with symbolism (particularly figurative language), which shows reader consider-ations
-Text -Hypertext -Graphic -Audio -Video	6: Overarching theme multilayered and complex; secondary themes integrally related to the primary themes	6: Round, dynamic major characters through rich description of affect, intention, and motivation	6: Setting fully integrated with the characters, action, and theme	6: Overarching problem and resolution supported by multiple episodes	6: Careful crafting of choic-es of story structure as well as vocabulary demonstrate considerate orchestration of all resources

(value), and (2) to inform, to a lesser extent, educational policy (utility). The positive results yielded in this study concerning the reliability and validity of the WWYR provide an avenue for teachers to accurately and consistently evaluate their students' hypermedia narrative productions by applying the WWYR assessment. The value of an assessment is the degree to which it enhances teacher instruction by linking teachers' comments to their instructional objectives (Wolf and Gearhart 1994). Therefore, in order for teachers to properly evaluate both student outcomes and the instructional effectiveness of their hypermedia/writing curricula, it is useful for all educators to apply a reliable and valid instrument. Furthermore, the positive correlation between the students' ITBS literacy skill score and WWYR average score for hypermedia productions indicated that students who were engaged in a hypermedia/writing curriculum improved their literacy skills.

NOTE

A couple of notes on correlations averaged across raters: (1) A relatively small number of raters (n = 5) were used in this study and the Gearhart, Herman, Novak, and Wolf (1995) study, which may have contributed to the lower r values across all subscales. The attenuation of correlational coefficients may be another explanation for the low levels of interrater reliability (Gay 1996). Accordingly, coefficients tend to be lower when a restricted range of values is uti-lized (e.g., the narrow range of only three out of a possible six WWYR subscale levels utilized by raters in this study). Thus, the more narrow the range of scores utilized by raters, the lower the coefficients. On the other hand, Gearhart et al. argued that if the number of raters was statistically increased fivefold, r values in the .50 to .60 range for Theme, Character, Setting, Plot, and Communication would be changed to .87, .89, .82, .86, and .89, respectively. Gearhart et al. used decision-study (multiplication of sample scores and aggregation of the results) coefficients to determine the number of raters needed to attain high reliability coefficients. (2) The r value for the Communication subscale in this study was considerably lower than the r value in the Gearhart et al. study (r = .50 versus .66). This sizable disparity in the level of interrater reliability may have been the result of the contrasting features of hypermedia-created narrative productions versus pen-and-paper-created narratives. The Communication subscale text primarily consisted of evaluative prompts designed to guide teachers in the assessment of writing style (see Table 4.1). Perhaps, in the current study, raters solely viewed textual features at the expense of the hypermedia features of graphics, sounds, buttons, and scanned art.

REFERENCES

Abedi, Jamal. "Final Report of Achievement, Section A." Report to the National Center for Education Statistics, contract no. RS90159001. Los Angeles: University of California, National Center for Research on Evaluation, Standards, and Student Testing, 1994.

Daiute, Colette, and Frances Morse. "Access to Knowledge and Expression: Multimedia Writing Tools for Students with Diverse Needs and Strengths." *Journal of Special Education Technology* 12, no. 3 (1994): 221–256.

Gay, Lorrie R. *Educational Research: Competencies for Analysis and Application.* 5th ed. Englewood Cliffs, NJ: Prentice-Hall, 1996.

Gearhart, Maryl, Joan L. Herman, John R. Novak, and Shelby A. Wolf. "Toward the Instructional Utility of Large-Scale Writing Assessment: Validation of a New Narrative Rubric." *Assessing Writing* 2, no. 2 (1995): 207–242.

Graves, Donald. *Writing: Teachers and Children at Work.* Portsmouth, NH: Heinemann, 1983.

International Reading Association (IRA) and National Council of Teachers of English (NCTE). *Standards for the English Language Arts.* Urbana, IL: NCTE; Newark, DE: IRA, 2001.

Linn, R., & Wilson, V. "Review of the Iowa Test of Basic Skills Form." In *Mental Measurement Yearbook,* 9th ed., edited by Jane Close Conoley and James C. Impara. Lincoln: University of Nebraska Press, 1990.

Messick, Stephen. "Validity of Test Interpretation and Use." In *Encyclopedia of Education Research,* 6th ed., edited by M. Alkin, 1487–1495. New York: Macmillan, 1992.

Mott, Michael S., and Jeanine Klomes. "The Synthesis of Writing Workshop and Hypermedia Authoring: Grades 1–4." *Early Childhood Research & Practice* 3, no. 2 (February 6, 2003). http://ecrp.illinois.edu/v3n2/mott.html.

Mott, Michael S., and William J. Sumrall. "Scientists Are Presenters: Tech Trek: Interactive Media." *Science Scope* 21, no. 7 (1998): 42–45.

Mott, Michael S., William J. Sumrall, and M. Lee Hodges. "Process and Computer-Based Elementary Writing Curriculum: A Review of Methods and Assessments." Paper presented at the Annual Meeting of the Mid-South Educational Research Association, Memphis, TN, November 1997.

Novak, John R., Joan L. Herman, and Maryl Gearhart. "Establishing Validity for Performance-Based Assessments: An Illustration for Collections of Student Writing." *Journal of Educational Research* 89, no. 4 (1996): 220–233.

Wagner, Roger. HyperStudio—presentation software. Palo Alto, CA: Roger Wagner Publishing, 1997–2001.

Wolf, Shelby A., and Maryl Gearhart. "Writing What You Read: A Framework for Narrative Assessment." *Language Arts* 71, no. 6 (1994): 425–445.

Yang, S. C. "A Dynamic Reading-Linking-to-Writing Model for Problem Solving Within a Constructive Hypermedia Learning Environment." *Journal of Educational Multimedia and Hypermedia* 5, no. 3/4 (1996): 263–283.

CREDITS

ASSESSMENT EXAMPLE 4. NARRATIVE WRITING RUBRIC FOR MEDIA (WWYR)

Interactive Assessment Work-Map

START HERE — 1

Directions

For the example assessment above you are now going to "interact" with it as you check off criteria and write brief statements and definitions about its general type and, specifically, its reliability, validity, value and utility technical characteristics. You are encouraged to infer how the assessment might be used in your own teaching if applicable.

2

How Is the Assessment Administered?

Individual ☐

Group ☐

3

Assessment, Test, Measurement, Evaluation Type

Note that an assessment can contain multiple types and/or degrees of type.

Test ☐ Achievement in what academic area/subject/domain? _____

Quiz ☐ For reinforcement/application or demonstrated understanding _____

Survey ☐ Cognitive and/or behavioral _____

Portfolio ☐ Collection of artifacts for learner demonstration of meeting various criteria and/or understanding _____

Inventory ☐ Collection of items/prompts for discernment of learning in a comprehensive manner, with all sub-elements of that area included _____

Artifact ☐ Specific evidence to learner demonstration of among various criteria and/or understanding _____

Exam ☐ Measuring specific content-area aligned to specific learning objectives _____

Case ☐ A specific unit of analysis or person with defined boundaries _____

Writing Prompt ☐ A query, question or directive to guide student writing _____

Content Area Performance/Presentation ☐ _____

4

Reliability and Validity

Reliable ☐

Valid *FOR WHAT PURPOSE?*
Describe assessment features that support the validity type/s identification.

-Face ☐

-Content ☐

-Criterion-related ☐

-Construct ☐

-Concurrent ☐

-Predictive ☐

-Developmental ☐

5

Qualities and Characteristics

Check each box that applies and briefly notate how the assessment meets these defined criteria for assessment purpose, making inferences from results and interpreting data.

☐ Static- _____ Dynamic ☐

☐ Developmental

☐ Vertical

☐ Formative _____ Summative ☐

☐ Value for Who/When/How?

-Student ☐
-Teacher ☐
-Parent ☐
-Administrator ☐
-Community ☐

Utility ☐ (Leading to specific Actions) _____

Interactive Assessment Work-Map developed by M. Mott (2016).

137

Interactive Assessment Work-Map NOTES

6

Reliability and Validity Description

Reliable ☐

Valid *FOR WHAT PURPOSE?* Describe assessment features that support the validity type/s identification. See information on validity definitions in the *Reliability, Validity, Value, and Utility* section of this book.

-Face ☐

-Content ☐

-Criterion-related ☐

-Construct ☐

-Concurrent ☐

-Predictive ☐

-Developmental ☐

Interactive Assessment Work-Map developed by M. Mott (2016).

Interactive Assessment Work-Map NOTES

Value and Utility

Discuss and describe the educational value of the assessment under review. What does it do? Who does it help and how? Why can it inform teaching and learning? Can it inform educational policy and leadership decision making? In what manner?

7

Value for ...?

Students ☐
-Content Area
-Cognitive
-Social-Emotional
-Teachers ☐
-Inform Instruction
-Formative
-Summative
-Dynamic

Utility for ...?

-Administrators ☐
-Support Supervision Goals and Policy
-Guide Schoolwide Efforts and Programming
-Parents and Community ☐
-Information for Parents on Status of Education

Interactive Assessment Work-Map developed by M. Mott (2016).

Interactive Assessment Work-Map NOTES

Applications to *Your Professional Practice*

8

Given the reliability, validity, value, and utility characteristics of the current assessment under review, discuss and describe how you would apply it in your professional practice. Hypothetically illustrate a reasoned use for the assessment and freely identify its strengths and limitations (validity issues) for making inferences from the results of the assessment for instruction.

Interactive Assessment Work-Map developed by M. Mott (2016).

ASSESSMENT EXAMPLE 5. ORAL READING FLUENCY SAMPLE

BACKGROUND

ORAL READING FLUENCY (ORF)

Oral Reading Fluency is a measure of reading skill that is related to the purpose for reading—understanding or comprehending text. ORF is thus a subcomponent of reading comprehension. According to Smith (1997), in order for reading to take place, the reader must read fluently, which contains three elements: (1) read accurately, with at least 95% of words read correctly; (2) the reader has to be fast so that the physiological short-term memory limitations of the brain do not function to make the reader forget what she has just read; and (3) the reader reads with expression, connecting text to layers of meaning, versus a

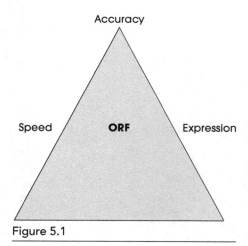

Figure 5.1

monotone without inflection, tone and pitch. Thus, ORF contains three vital elements (see Figure 5.1).

Fluency is not to be mistaken for comprehension (or how a reader understands and makes sense of text), but it is a critical bridge to comprehension in that accurate reading that is fast and full of expression facilitates understanding. ORF is one the five components of literacy as defined by the congressionally appointed National Reading Panel (2012), and it is a part of the reading curriculum taught by Pre-K–12 grade teachers, albeit stressed in grades 1–5, where reading skills are developed.

Oral Reading Fluency is assessed via a relatively simple process. An individual student reads a passage orally to the teacher/assessor. The passage has been "leveled" by a process called Lexile Measure (https://lexile.com/), which provides information (such as mean sentence length, mean log word frequency, and word count) on how complex the passage is. In this way the teacher can, at first, estimate appropriate text to have the student read at first. For example, if you have a second grader who is "advanced" at reading, the teacher may choose a passage with a Lexile Measure equating to third grade.

ORF scores are measured by WCPM—words read correctly per minute while recording accuracy, speed, and expression. The teacher has the student read a passage that has a set amount of words and, using a timer, she times the reading for two minutes. At the close of two minutes, total WCPM is calculated by counting the words read during that two-minute time span. Errors are noted (see ORF Directions) as well as expression, using a simple qualitative rubric delineating (a) expression; (b) smoothness; and (c) phrasing based upon punctuation.

SELECTING THE PROPER TEXT/ PASSAGE FOR THE STUDENT

Some readers and reading passages are leveled with the Lexile Measure of text complexity available at https://lexile.com/. However, if your passage does not have an accompanying Lexile level for you to determine a match for your reader, you can enter the passage (if you have digital access to it) into the Lexile leveler on their free resource page for educators. The important aspect about matching text to reader is to find the level at which they can read fluently, even if it is above or below their grade level.

GRADE LEVEL–LEXILE MEASURE CHART[1]

1	Up to 280L
2	230L to 580L
3	360L to 720L
4	480L to 830L
5	620L to 950L
6	690L to 1020L
7	780L to 1090L
8	820L to 1140L
9	880L to 1180L
10	920L to 1200L
11	940L to 1210L
12	950L to 1220L

---

1 *Common Core State Standards for English Language Art and Literacy in History/Social Studies, Science, and Technical Subjects: Appendix A.* http://www.corestandards.org/assets/Appendix_A.pdf

ORF DIRECTIONS FOR THE PASSAGE FROM ADRIFT IN THE WILDS; OR, THE ADVENTURES OF TWO SHIPWRECKED BOYS [2]

In a quiet area in the classroom, explain to the student, "I am going to learn more about how you read so that I can teach you effectively. Relax, take your time, and read the following passage, and I am going to take notes." The teacher notes that the Lexile level of 1020L (see Grade Level–Lexile Measure Chart) corresponds to a sixth-grade level of text complexity, and since Student A is an advanced fifth grader, she starts with text one grade level up (note that the text you select might be too easy or too difficult; in this case, you simply stop and select a different text/level).

A.   Set your timer at the two-minute mark.

B.   Ask the student to read the Student Version passage "as best as you can."

C.   Begin by stating "you may read now" and hit the timer button (iPhone timer/Android timer is usually used).

D.   While the student reads, the assessor marks miscues onto the Teacher Version of the passage.

    a.   Incorrectly read word: "I"

    b.   Insertion: "Ins"

    c.   Not read or Deletion: "Del"

    d.   Punctuation use

    e.   Expression (tone, pitch, etc.)

---

2   Edward S. Ellis, Selection from Chapter I, *Adrift in the Wilds; or, The Adventures of Two Shipwrecked Boys.* Copyright in the Public Domain.

E. Scoring

a. Final Fluency Score = Number of words read correctly per minute divided by any miscues that change the meaning of the word.

b. Expression: Low, Medium, and High. This is qualitative, based upon the subjective viewpoint of the assessor. Low would be reading with little inflection, punctuation use, and change in pitch and tone of voice. Medium would be some use of those categories, and High would be full use of all elements of expression.

STUDENT VERSION—SHIPWRECKED BOYS[3]

One beautiful midsummer night in 1888, a large, heavily laden steamer was making her way swiftly up the Pacific coast, in the direction of San Francisco. She was opposite the California shore, only a day's sail distant from the City of the Golden Gate, and many of the passengers had already begun making preparations for landing, even though a whole night and the better part of a day was to intervene ere they could expect to set their feet upon solid land.

She was one of those magnificent steamers that ply regularly between Panama and California. She had rather more than her full cargo of freight and passengers; but, among the hundreds of the latter, we have to do with but three.

On this moonlight night, there were gathered by themselves these three personages, consisting of Tim O'Rooney, Elwood Brandon and Howard Lawrence. The first was a burly, good-natured Irishman, and the two latter were cousins, their ages differing by less than a month, and both being in their sixteenth year.

The financial storm that swept over the country in 1888, toppling down merchants and banking-houses like so many ten-pins, carried with it in the general wreck and ruin, that of Brandon, Herman & Co., and the senior partner, Sylvanus Brandon, returned to his home in Brooklyn, New York, one evening worse than penniless.

While he was meditating, dejected and gloomy, as to the means by which he was to keep the wolf from the door, his clerk brought him a letter which had been overlooked in the afternoon's mail, postmarked, "San Francisco, Cal." At once he recognized the bold, handsome superscription as that of his kind-hearted brother-in-law, Thomas Lawrence. His heart beat with a strong hope as he broke the envelope, and his eyes glistened ere he had read one-half.

TEACHER VERSION—SHIPWRECKED BOYS

LEXILE LEVELING

- Lexile Measure
- 1020L
- Mean Sentence Length
- 27.55
- Mean Log Word Frequency
- 3.55
- Word Count
- 303

---

3 Public domain source: https://www.gutenberg.org/files/21626/21626-h/21626-h.htm#CHAPTER_I.

One beautiful midsummer night in 1888, a large, heavily laden steamer was making her way swiftly up the Pacific coast, in the direction of San Francisco. She was opposite the California shore, only a day's sail distant from the City of the Golden Gate, and many of the passengers had already begun making preparations for landing, even though a whole night and the better part of a day was to intervene ere they could expect to set their feet upon solid land.	1 2 3 4 5 6 7 8 9 10 11 12
She was one of those magnificent steamers that ply regularly between Panama and California. She had rather more than her full cargo of freight and passengers; but, among the hundreds of the latter, we have to do with but three.	13 14 15 16 17 18

On this moonlight night, there were gathered by themselves these three personages, consisting of Tim O'Rooney, Elwood Brandon and Howard Lawrence. The first was a burly, good-natured Irishman, and the two latter were cousins, their ages differing by less than a month, and both being in their sixteenth year.

The financial storm that swept over the country in 1888, toppling down merchants and banking-houses like so many ten-pins, carried with it in the general wreck and ruin, that of Brandon, Herman & Co., and the senior partner, Sylvanus Brandon, returned to his home in Brooklyn, New York, one evening worse than penniless.

While he was meditating, dejected and gloomy, as to the means by which he was to keep the wolf from the door, his clerk brought him a letter which had been overlooked in the afternoon's mail, postmarked, "San Francisco, Cal." At once he recognized the bold, handsome superscription as that of his kind-hearted brother-in-law, Thomas Lawrence. His heart beat with a strong hope as he broke the envelope, and his eyes glistened ere he had read one-half.

ANALYSIS OF RESULTS

In the right-hand column, note reading miscues; if a miscue does not lead to a change in text comprehension, you do not count this as an error. Follow the directions in the section prior to this one to determine the ORF level of the student. There are three goals of ORF assessment: (1) determine reading speed at various levels of text complexity, (2) measure accuracy of reading, and (3) qualitatively determine the level of expression of the reading. For all three categories, the ORF results will point to teacher instructional decision making and the creation of specific learning objectives. For example:

1   The student is in third grade, but for independent reading (95% accuracy for comprehension), the student needs books with a Lexile level equivalent to second grade.

2   Miscues (words read incorrectly that changed the meaning of the text) occurred in words with within-word complexity involving advanced vowel generalizations such

"igh" and "oi" or "ea," which points to specific instructional objectives addressing advanced vowel spellings.

3   Expression was low, given the lack of attention to punctuation and variance in pitch and tone of voice, leading the teacher to design lessons focusing on expression guided by punctuation and the meanings addressed in the story.

Interactive Assessment Work-Map

Directions

START HERE

1

For the example assessment above you are now going to "interact" with it as you check off criteria and write brief statements and definitions about its general type and, specifically, its reliability, validity, value and utility technical characteristics. You are encouraged to infer how the assessment might be used in your own teaching if applicable.

2 ✎

How Is the Assessment Administered?

Individual ☐

Group ☐

3

Assessment, Test, Measurement, Evaluation Type

Note that an assessment can contain multiple types and/or degrees of types.

Test ☐ Achievement in what academic area/subject/domain?
_____

Quiz ☐ For reinforcement/application or demonstrated understanding _____

Survey ☐ Cognitive and/or behavioral

Portfolio ☐ Collection of artifacts for learner demonstration of meeting various criteria and/or understanding

Inventory ☐ Collection of items/prompts for discernment of learning in a comprehensive manner, with all sub-elements of that area included _____

Artifact ☐ Specific evidence to learner demonstration of among various criteria and/or understanding

Exam ☐ Measuring specific content-area aligned to specific learning objectives _____

Case ☐ A specific unit of analysis or person with defined boundaries

Writing Prompt ☐ A query, question or directive to guide student writing _____

Content Area Performance/Presentation ☐ _____

Qualities and Characteristics

Check each box that applies and briefly notate how the assessment meets these defined criteria for assessment purpose, making inferences from results and interpreting data.

☐ Static- _____ Dynamic ☐

☐ Developmental

☐ Vertical

☐ Formative _____ Summative ☐

☐ Value for Who/When/How?

-Student ☐
-Teacher ☐
-Parent ☐
-Administrator ☐
-Community ☐

Utility ☐ (Leading to specific Actions) _____

5

4

Reliability and Validity

Reliable ☐

- - - - - - - - - - - - - - -

Valid *FOR WHAT PURPOSE?*
Describe assessment features that support the validity type/s identification.

-Face ☐

-Content ☐

-Criterion-related ☐

-Construct ☐

-Concurrent ☐

-Predictive ☐

-Developmental ☐

Interactive Assessment Work-Map developed by M. Mott (2016).

Interactive Assessment Work-Map NOTES

6

Reliability and Validity Description

Reliable ☐

Valid **FOR WHAT PURPOSE?** *Describe assessment features that support the validity type/s identification. See information on validity definitions in the Reliability, Validity, Value, and Utility section of this book.*

-Face ☐

-Content ☐

-Criterion-related ☐

-Construct ☐

-Concurrent ☐

-Predictive ☐

-Developmental ☐

Interactive Assessment Work-Map developed by M. Mott (2016).

Interactive Assessment Work-Map NOTES

Value and Utility

Discuss and describe the educational value of the assessment under review. What does it do? Who does it help and how? Why can it inform teaching and learning? Can it inform educational policy and leadership decision making? In what manner?

7

Value for ...?

Students ☐
-Content Area
-Cognitive
-Social-Emotional

-Teachers ☐
-Inform Instruction
-Formative
-Summative
-Dynamic

Utility for ...?

-Administrators ☐
-Support Supervision Goals and Policy
-Guide Schoolwide Efforts and Programming

-Parents and Community ☐
-Information for Parents on Status of Education

Interactive Assessment Work-Map developed by M. Mott (2016).

Interactive Assessment Work-Map NOTES

Applications to *Your Professional Practice*

8

Given the reliability, validity, value, and utility characteristics of the current assessment under review, discuss and describe how you would apply it in your professional practice. Hypothetically illustrate a reasoned use for the assessment and freely identify its strengths and limitations (validity issues) for making inferences from the results of the assessment for instruction.

ASSESSMENT EXAMPLE 6. MEDIA-ENHANCED SCIENCE PRESENTATION RUBRIC (MESPR)

ASSESSING STUDENT SCIENTIFIC EXPRESSION USING MEDIA:

THE MEDIA-ENHANCED SCIENCE PRESENTATION RUBRIC (MESPR)[1]

INTRODUCTION

The very notion of "writing" and "presenting" is increasingly being transformed by new digital media used daily in society in general and in homes, businesses, and schools. Today, one's ability to represent thought digitally with a variety of media is

1 From Mott, Sumrall, Rutherford, and Moore, "Assessing Student Scientific Expression Using Media: The Media Enhanced Science Presentation Rubric," *Journal of STEM Education, Innovations, and Research*, 12, no. 1 (2011): 33–41. Reproduced with permission from Dr. P. K. Raju, Editor in Chief of the *Journal of STEM Education, Innovations, and Research*.

more important than ever. The extreme pace of transformation in society, represented by new technology, from PDAs to creative software applications for an assortment of devices, dictates that K–12 educators consider how to facilitate science education that supports students as they express themselves digitally in various environments in developmentally appropriate ways. This article addresses the curriculum, instruction, and assessment of students' digitally-enhanced science experiment results and includes a rubric that supports teacher-to-student dialogue and student-to-student dialogue on the incorporation of text, audio, video, and graphics in science presentations. The Media-Enhanced Science Presentation Rubric (MESPR) is defined and its use is discussed, with the goal of improving student understanding of both the scientific method and science literacy skills.

RATIONALE FOR THE NEED FOR A SCIENCE PRESENTATION RUBRIC

As science and science literacy curricula and instruction continue to transform to include new digital communication and learning environments, educators must correspondingly develop and technically evaluate assessments for the new environments. Digital media represents a powerful electronic environment through which science literacy and expression can be facilitated by the manipulation of text, graphics, audio, and video elements, and this technology and integration are reflected in the latest science literacy and literacy K–12 standards (American Association for the Advancement of Science 2009; Hague and Mason 1986). The qualities of digital media that support higher-level cognitive processes such as synthesis, organization, evaluation, and reflexivity have been well documented (Mott and Benus 2006; Moot, Etsler, and Drumgold 2013; Yang 1996). However, there is a glaring absence of methods and tools to assess students' media-enhanced products. To address this absence, a scientific method process was merged with a framework for digital media inclusion.

These terms are defined as follows:

- Digital media (McChesney 2007):

  digital communication technologies that enable or facilitate user-to-user interactivity and interactivity between user and information. Media also refers to the mode of communication, and this can include any combination of digital and seamless connections between text and other meaning-based symbol systems.

- Digital media contains two main components:
  (1) digital: the ability to program electronic links, or hyperconnections, to connect information to any other Internet-based source or simply to link locally to an electronic device, and
  (2) media: the ability to manipulate multiple meaning-based symbol systems representing a variety of sources—text, graphics, audio, and video clips.

As students are increasingly required and expected to incorporate a variety of sources in a sometimes-dizzying array of digital modes, never has it been more critical for educators to structure the manner in which students synthesize science experiment results and information to better yield convincing and organized science presentation result products. This article does not address the presentation software due to the fact that educator preference usually reigns in terms of decision making over authorware. Whether or not students author in PowerPoint, SmartNotebook, Dreamweaver, etc. has no bearing on how teachers separately and eventually assess student science experiment results. For assistance on authoring with digital media, there are numerous sources available for teachers to separately teach skill sets required to use Microsoft and other publisher materials (see Mott and Benus 2006 for further assistance).

THE MESPR

The Media-Enhanced Science Presentation Rubric serves three purposes: (a) promote student understanding of the scientific method, with the overall aim of empowering students to conduct inquiry-based hands-on science experiments; (b) empower students to logically incorporate digital media elements to further promote understanding of their scientific experiment results; and (c) foster communication skills and "habits of mind" in science. According to Project 2061, science, mathematics, and technology share certain thinking-process skills essential for science literacy. "Habits of mind" in science incorporate these skills and, in addition, consider value and attitudes toward science. These goals have been articulated by AAAS in the science standards from Project 2061 in the "methods" and "technology" strands (http://www.project2061.org/publications/bsl/online/index.php) and in Chapter 12, "Habits of Mind" (http://www.project2061.org/publications/sfaa/online/chap12.htm). Thus, three core knowledge and processes areas addressed in the benchmark are holistically infused in the rubric to promote student activity that leads to their involvement in the scientific method and technological ability to express their work. The first, "enhanced media," deals with student understanding of the nature of technology and the need for dissemination as addressed in the standards:

> *... technology extends our abilities to change the world: to cut, shape, or put together materials; to move things from one place to another; to reach farther with our hands, voices, and senses. We use technology to try to change the world to suit us better. ... Anticipating the effects of technology is therefore as important as advancing its capabilities (3A–C).*

> *The dissemination of scientific information is crucial to its progress. Some scientists present their findings and theories in papers that are delivered at meetings or published in scientific journals 1C/H12 (American Association for the Advancement of Science 2009).*

The second core knowledge area holistically addressed across elementary and secondary grade ranges is the makeup of the scientific method. Project 2061 addresses this understanding from a developmental standpoint: in this example, Grades 3–5:

> *They should be encouraged to observe more and more carefully, measure things with increasing accuracy (where the nature of the investigations involves measurement), record data clearly in logs and journals, and communicate their results in charts and simple graphs as well as in prose. Time should be provided to let students run enough trials to be confident of their results. Investigations should often be followed up with presentations to the entire class to emphasize the importance of clear communication in science. Class discussions of the procedures and findings can provide the beginnings of scientific argument and debate (1B, Grades 3–5) (American Association for the Advancement of Science 2009).*

The third core knowledge/skills area holistically addressed across K–12 is the "convention style" discourse where presenters, peers, and instructor engage in posing questions, analyzing and evaluating the scientific investigation, offering critique, and discussing extensions of the research. Through this process, "habits of mind" in science become another focal point around which to promote social values of science and technology and reflect on students' own ability to understand and analyze science content and processes (http://www.project2061. org/publications/sfaa/online/chap12.htm).

The above examples of science goals for technology, dissemination and method/inquiry, and "habits of mind" can be adapted for both emergent and advanced science students. Likewise, the rubric must be adapted to meet the developmental levels of students' science and literacy capabilities. The rubric contains the superordinate concepts of the discrete stages of the scientific method across the top row, with the media elements explicitly identified in the left column and embedded in the narrative descriptions in the cells. (See Table 6.1, The

MESPR: MEDIA-ENHANCED SCIENCE EXPERIMENT PRESENTATION RUBRIC

Score / Criteria	Problem/ Question	Hypothesis	Material/ Methods	Results/ Analyses	Conclusions/ Further Investigation	Communication Skills
1	Either not present or incorrectly written; no connection to experiment. Does not connect with valid society and technology issue *Use of relevant media is marginal* *Hypertext: does not link to supporting texts*	Not present and/or incorrectly conveyed *Use of relevant media is marginal* *Graphics: designed to visually depict variables to support text are not present (when appropriate to the variable types ...)*	Not included and/or incomplete. Mostly "cookbook" style project. No quantification of data *Minimal attempt to use relevant or contributory media* *Hypertext: not used to link to additional material descriptions or methods used by other scientists* *Graphics: not present to visually portray materials and method steps* *Audio: supporting audio not present to provide additional description of materials and methods* *Video: supporting video (clips) not present to portray methods applied during the experiment*	Not included and/or incomplete. Use of relevant or contributory media is marginal. Details on data collection are not presented (examples from logbook) *Does not attempt to create an online logbook* *Text: minimal or no use of text style to structure text elements of superordinate to subordinate concepts* *Hypertext: minimal or no use of links to support results and analyses* *Graphics: minimal visuals to support and model findings* *Audio: minimal or no audio to support and model findings (if appropriate to this experiment and this section)* *Video: minimal or no video to support and model findings (if appropriate to this experiment and this section)*	Incomplete – no connection with results and to further investigations. No connection with society or technology issues *Use of relevant or contributory media is marginal. Incorrect use of terminology and science, e.g., my results "proved" I was right or "I didn't get the results I expected"* *Minimal use of text, hypertext, graphics, audio and video elements lead to summarizing findings across multiple meaning-based symbol systems to make complex information easier to understanding*	Demonstrates little depth or understanding of project, reads directly from notes, is unable to field questions and engage in critical dialogue. Demonstrates little interest or curiosity in topic. No mention of logbook or data collection details *Doesn't use media in a relevant or contributory way. No connections to society or technology*
2	One element is not present or is incorrectly written. Some connection with society and technology issue *Makes adequate use of media.* *Hypertext: links relate to and support the readers' understanding of the experiment problem* *Graphics, Audio and Video: Elements depict problem visually*	Present but incomplete connection between independent & dependent variables. No operational definition *Use of relevant media somewhat conveys concepts.* *Graphics: designed to visually depict variables to support text are present when*	Both materials and methods included with some creativity. Limited quantification of data *Some use of media to convey this step and methods processes* *Hypertext: used to link to additional material descriptions or methods used by other scientists* *Graphics: present to visually portray materials and method steps* *Audio: supporting audio present to provide additional description of*	Both aspects included. Marginally complete content or use of relevant and contributory media *Some effort at creating online logbook.* *Text: adequate use of text style to structure text elements of superordinate to subordinate concepts* *Hypertext: adequate use of links to support results and analyses* *Graphics: visuals function to support and model findings* *Audio: functions to support and model findings (if appropriate to this experiment and this*	Both aspects included with adequate connection to result and analysis *Minimal connection to society or technology issues. Partially correct use of terms and science, "My results supported my hypothesis" but doesn't value unexpected observations* *Adequate use of text, hypertext, graphics, audio and video elements lead to summarizing findings across multiple meaning-based symbol systems to make complex information easier to understanding*	Adequate depth of understanding; fields some questions, Refers to logbook and data collection details demonstrates some curiosity or interest *Media is used marginally to contribute in a relevant manner. Some connections to society or technology*

Table 6.1. The Media-Enhanced Science Experiment Presentation Rubric (MESPR).

| 3 | Both problem statement and question are present correctly conveyed and relate to experiment. Clear connection to society and technology issue

Creative and clear use of media to enhance

Hypertext: links relate to and convincingly support the readers' understanding of the experiment problem

Graphics, Audio and Video: Elements depict problem visually increasing audience understanding | Correctly connects independent with independent variables. Operational definitions present.

Creative use of media to present concepts

Graphics: designed to visually depict variables to support variables are present and convincingly aide reader under standing of variables and similarities/ differences between variables (when appropriate to the variable types ...) | Materials and methods included completely and creatively. Quantification of data appropriate to the methodology utilized

Media is fully utilized in a creative way convey the information

Hypertext: used to ink to additional material descriptions or methods used by other scientists

Graphics: present to visually portray materials and method steps

Audio: supporting audio present to provide additional description of materials and methods

Video: supporting video (clips) present to portray methods applied during the experiment | Both aspects included completely. Excellent use online logbook with creative and illuminating use of media to present information and to engage audience.

Details on data collection are included and fully integrated into presentation

Text: aesthetically convincing use of text style to structure text elements of superordinate to subordinate concepts

Hypertext: convincing use of links to support results and analyses to increase audience understanding of the project

Graphics: support and model findings enabling the audience to scale down the complexity of the project

Audio: convincingly support and model findings (if appropriate to this experiment and this section)

Video: convincingly support and model findings (if appropriate to this experiment and this section) | Both aspects included completely with excellent correlation to results and analysis.

Creative and illuminating use of media to present information and to engage audience. Correct use of terms and values unexpected observations

Convincing use of text, hypertext, graphics, audio and video elements lead to summarizing findings across multiple meaningbased symbol systems to make complex information easier to understanding | Good depth of understanding, enthusiastically fields questions and demonstrates curiosity and interest in topic. Integrates aspects of logbook confidently and appropriately, Engages audience and stimulates a lively discussion

Creative and relevant use of media to convey ideas. Good connections to society or technology |

Table 6.1. The Media-Enhanced Science Experiment Presentation Rubric (MESPR). (Continued)

Media-Enhanced Science Presentation Rubric.) The text within cells is designed to promote discussion between student and teacher and between students along the educational objectives for science method and science literacy with media. The authors seek to promote classroom discussion based upon science goals versus merely along grade levels and "points" earned. The narrative quality of the rubric thus supports a deeper understanding of emergent-to-advanced goals for students as they conduct research and present their findings. Similar to holistic writing rubrics validated for collections of student narrative writing samples (see Novak, Herman, and Gearhart 1996), this rubric is thus a formative and performance-based tool that can guide teacher and student language and increase student meta-awareness of what a science presentation with media can accomplish.

The MESPR supports the National Science Education Standards (National Research Council 1996) teaching standards, as it encourages teachers to develop short-term and long-term goals facilitating students' skills of inquiry, "orchestrate discourse among students about scientific ideas ..." (p. 32), and "guide students in self-assessment" (p. 38). Through communicating their inquiry investigations, students can use the criteria developed in the MESPR to enhance self-directed and reflective learning. The NSES recommends that teachers "make the available science tools, materials, and technological resources accessible to students," (p. 44) and the MESPR is an effective evaluation tool to assess student competence in using these resources to enhance content, process, and attitude in an inquiry-based program.

FACE VALIDITY OF RATER JUDGMENTS OF STUDENT SCIENCE PRESENTATION QUALITY

Utilizing Messick's (Messick 1996: 1992) holistic conception of validity (the degree to which an instrument measures what it purports to measure), the authors (five higher education science and literacy educators with doctorates) evaluated the face validity of the rubric. Face validity is a subcomponent of construct validity, which is the degree to which an instrument measures a uni- or multidimensional construct of a body of knowledge—in this case, the scientific method and science literacy (Messick 1996). For the current article, the authors/content-area experts assessed the face validity of the MESPR for the multidimensional construct of (a) scientific method and (b) digitally enhanced science literacy. The science and literacy experts (n = 5) qualitatively evaluated the rubric in three ways:

1   They analyzed the rubric for alignment with AAAS Project 2061 science education standards to discern the relationship between research-based goals articulated in the standards and their iteration with the rubric narrative descriptions;

2   They determined that the scientific method descriptions and levels were appropriate for an elementary and secondary audience and indeed addressed the structure of scientific inquiry; and

3   The rubric cell descriptions were open-ended enough to support a variety of scientific investigations and use of a wide array of digital media.

RESULTS AND DISCUSSION

The MESPR provides a scaffold or tool that enables students to focus on presenting a science project where they must synthesize the scientific inquiry model and scientific processes into a coherent presentation using various media formats. Friedman (2005) identifies eight roles that individuals will need to participate in the flattened world. Two of these roles are the synthesizer and adapter. The synthesizer is able to see relationships between unrelated phenomena to form one idea or entity. The other role, leverager, describes individuals who can self-monitor or self-assess in order to meet the continuously changing workplace demands by using an inquiry model (identifying a problem, analyzing, solving, and redesigning) to solve problems in ways that others can replicate.

Another set of benchmarks to which the rubric shows strong alignment is the nature of technology and the designed world. As students integrate digital technologies into the presentation, they are gaining valuable experience in using technology to communicate ideas in a responsible manner that follows scientific procedures. The rubric is also aligned with the AAAS Project 2061 benchmarks "Common Themes" and "Habits of Mind." As students complete the scientific inquiry process and report results, the rubric focuses students' attention on being able to explain some of the common themes found in the benchmarks and being able to develop those scientific habits of mind necessary for becoming productive members of the ever-changing society and workplace. Finally, as students choose their own inquiry topics, they will meet other benchmarks (e.g., "The Living Environment," "The Human Organism," "Human Society") distinctive to their focus area.

The final criteria for determining face validity focuses on whether descriptions are open-ended enough to support a variety of scientific investigations and use of a wide array of digital media. The descriptions within the rubric are open-ended to the degree that the scientific inquiry model allows. There are certain characteristics inherently necessary to be included within the descriptors that characterize this model. The rubric also allows students flexibility in using a wide array of digital media to communicate their projects to a specific audience in a professional manner. In thinking about the aforementioned roles described by Friedman (2005), students are afforded the opportunity to use digital media to enhance their science presentations that will better prepare them to live in the "flat world" described by Friedman.

TEACHING AND LEARNING VALUE AND UTILITY OF THE MESPR

The value of an assessment is the degree to which it enhances the minute-by-minute interactions in the classroom by aligning learning goals with discussions pointed to achieving those goals. The utility of an assessment relates to the extent to which results correlate with science experiment learning goals. As teachers search for creative ways to engage students in the learning process, the MESPR contains value for facilitating science inquiry in the following ways: (a) it provides a formal document where teachers are able to communicate their expectations for the presentation; (b) it provides the necessary information so that students understand the criteria for designing a presentation that meets the standards; and (c) it provides a framework for students to assess their own performance, focusing the locus of control and ownership of work on the student. Nicol and Macfarlane-Dick (2006) describe five principles that support the use of formative assessments like the MESPR. The assessment:

1   Helps clarify what good performance is (goals, criteria, expected standards)

2   Facilitates the development of self-assessment (reflection) in learning

3   Delivers high-quality information to students about their learning

4   Encourages teacher and peer dialogue around learning

5   Provides information that teachers can use to help shape teaching" (p. 205).

These principles certainly apply to teacher and peer feedback that can be given using the MESPR, as well as self-assessment and reflection.

National and state standards incorporating technology are increasingly required, and the MESPR incorporates novel digital media as a tool for motivating students to engage in the learning process. This alignment with standards provides evidence of assessment utility. When students are given opportunities to use out-of-school literacies (e.g., web development, wiki, blog, social networking) that use digital media, they are more engaged and motivated in the learning process (Alvermann and McLean 2007; Hull and Zacher 2009; International Reading Association and National Council of Teachers in English 1996; Prensky 2001; Tierney, Bond, and Bresler 2006). In addition to fostering connections to out-of-school literacies, the rubric serves as a scaffold where students are able to make choices about the media included in their presentation.

PROMOTING LITERACY (AND SCIENCE LITERACY)

The MESPR provides students with a myriad of ways to highlight their literate lives. Students are engaged in many literate activities outside of school that promote literacy competency. Too often, in-school literacy tasks do not mirror the ways that students use literacy in their everyday lives (Dunston and Gambrell 2009). Thus, the MESPR allows students to demonstrate their out-of-school expertise in their science courses. Another way that the MESPR highlights students' literacy is that it allows students to build on their multiliterate communication abilities using an array of digital media. Designing presentations described in the MESPR, students showcase their technological, visual, media, and information literacy skills. Using these "multiliteracies," a term coined by the New London Group students "discover voice, confidence, and structure in their writing" (Sylvester and Greenidge 2009). The MESPR also provides an avenue through which students can collaborate with peers as they seek peer feedback related to the creation of their presentation. This collaboration captures high levels of literate discussion related to the multiliteracies cited above. Students' experiences may foster a new "respect for classmates and their opinions, understanding work team dynamics, and using them for high-quality outcomes, taking turns, recognizing the different learning that can occur in the collaborative and cooperative context" (Afflerback 2007).

In considering how the MESPR aligns with National Council of Teachers of English (NCTE) and International Reading Association (IRA) Standards for the English Language Arts[2] several connections are evident. Specifically, Standards 1, 3–8, 11, and 12 most parallel with MESPR and the literacy processes required to design and implement the presentation. Some of the Standards (Hague and Mason 1986) are listed below.

- Standard 1: Students read a wide range of print and non-print texts to build an understanding of texts, of themselves, and of the cultures of the United States and the world; to acquire new information; to respond to the needs and demands of society and the workplace; and for personal fulfillment. Among these texts are fiction and nonfiction, classic and contemporary works.

- Standard 3: Students apply a wide range of strategies to comprehend, interpret, evaluate, and appreciate texts. They draw on their prior experience, their interactions with other readers and writers, their knowledge of word meaning and of other texts, their word identification strategies, and their understanding of textual features (e.g., sound-letter correspondence, sentence structure, context, graphics).

- Standard 4: Students adjust their use of spoken, written, and visual language (e.g., conventions, style, vocabulary) to communicate effectively with a variety of audiences and for different purposes.

- Standard 5: Students employ a wide range of strategies as they write and use different writing process elements appropriately to communicate with different audiences for a variety of purposes.

- Standard 6: Students apply knowledge of language structure, language conventions (e.g., spelling and punctuation), media techniques, figurative language, and genre to create, critique, and discuss print and non-print texts.

- Standard 7: Students conduct research on issues and interests by generating ideas and questions, and by posing problems. They gather, evaluate, and synthesize data from a variety of sources (e.g., print and non-print texts, artifacts, people) to communicate their discoveries in ways that suit their purpose and audience.

- Standard 8: Students use a variety of technological and information resources (e.g., libraries, databases, computer networks, video) to gather and synthesize information and to create and communicate knowledge.

---

2 Standards for the English Language Arts, by the International Reading Association and the National Council of Teachers of English, Copyright 1996 by the International Reading Association and the National Council of Teachers of English. Reprinted with permission.

- Standard 11: Students participate as knowledgeable, reflective, creative, and critical members of a variety of literacy communities.
- Standard 12: Students use spoken, written, and visual language to accomplish their own purposes (e.g., for learning, enjoyment, persuasion, and the exchange of information) (Hague and Mason 1986).

In addition, the Partnership for 21st Century Skills (2003) identifies learning skills relevant for students who will job search with individuals in a highly competitive global society, or flattened world, as described by Freidman (2005). The Partnership describes three discrete categories of skills: information and communication skills, thinking and problem-solving skills, and interpersonal and self-directional skills. The MESPR supplies a structure for designing the presentation that fosters students' development in these key skills identified as crucial for student success in the global workplace.

CONCLUSIONS

In the current paper, the authors have identified several attributes inherent to the MESPR as a tool for promoting teacher–student and student–student interaction along science methods and science literacy understanding. The National Science Education Standards (1996) has made the call for science educators to address these underutilized educationally important areas:

> Everyone needs to use scientific information to make choices that arise every day. Everyone needs to be able to engage intelligently in public discourse and debate about important issues that involve science and technology. And everyone deserves to share in the excitement and personal fulfillment that can come from understanding and learning about the natural world.

The importance for our future democracy of educating students literate in science cannot be underestimated:

> Scientific literacy also is of increasing importance in the workplace. More and more jobs demand advanced skills, requiring that people be able to learn, reason, think creatively, make decisions, and solve problems. An understanding of science and the processes of science contributes in an essential way to these skills. Other countries are investing heavily to create scientifically and technically literate work forces.

Therefore, the need to address technology at all grade levels is crucial. Technology "involves the purposeful application of knowledge, experience, and resources to create products and processes that meet human needs" (Curriculum Corporation 1993). Many times, children take technology for granted, or they may not be aware of what constitutes technology or a tool. When design and technology are incorporated into the science curriculum, students are more likely to become natural explorers. The students can channel their creative impulses to express ideas, solve problems, and present their findings to others in creative ways as they integrate digital media into their presentations. Using the Media-Enhanced Science Presentation Rubric (MESPR) will promote creative expression and problem solving by having the students model scientific thinking and share observations through the use of technology that will better prepare them for the workforce.

As teachers use the MESPR, they will have the opportunity to observe and question students about their work. Teacher guidance will help students consider what is reasonable and possible. According to the American Association of Science (2009) the discussions necessary to make decisions are part of the design process and teach students about the "'*constraints*' involved whenever a project is to be undertaken" (p. 49). Teachers will be able to observe the learning process, and through these observations, the teacher's knowledge about students and what they are learning will be richer and more comprehensive.

Dodge, Jablon, and Bickart (1994), in *Constructing Curriculum for the Primary Grades*, stated that giving students a chance to apply knowledge they have gained during a study by building a model, making a presentation, or building an exhibit helps them synthesize what they have learned and feel proud of the work they have done. Media-enhanced science presentations are perfect for sharing their knowledge about a topic with family members and members of a larger community.

The MESPR rubric cell descriptions were open-ended to support a variety of scientific investigations. According to the National Science Education Standards over the course of grades K–4, student investigations and design problems should incorporate more than one material and several contexts in science and technology. Experiences should be complemented by observation and analysis skills using a sequence of stages: stating the problem, designing the approach, implementing the solution, evaluating the solution, and communicating the problem, design, and solution. The MESPR would serve to further enhance communicating the problem, design, and solution. The students could include text, hypertext, graphic, audio, and/or video to accentuate their experiences. Furthermore, students can incorporate and explore many different forms of technology and tools that scientists use to enhance their knowledge and broaden their inventive energy in school and later in the workforce!

Further research is recommended to technically examine the presence of other validity qualities of the MESPR for assessing student science presentations and determining the degree to which high performance on the MESPR is correlated with other high performance on science literacy tasks. Significant results might bridge the divide between instruments with high classroom value and utility for teaching and learning to norm-referenced measures used to advise science education policy makers.

STUDENT RESPONSES TO THE MESPR

In an effort to incorporate feedback about the use of the MESPR from students, the authors gathered responses from teacher education candidates about their use of the rubric in an undergraduate science methods course to better understand how to communicate with in-service teachers in professional development efforts. Selected comments from students are paraphrased:

1   The rubric columns are easy to figure out, as the scientific method components are clear and straightforward.

2   The media elements seem very high level and would require training to accomplish.

3   Students, in all probability, would require extra technology training in addition to having to learn about the scientific method.

4   Younger students may not have the competencies to convey ideas at the top levels of the rubric.

5   The rubric "helps me to understand what to teach and to talk to the kids about …" and seems like it would be appropriate for science fair projects developed over time.

6   Experiencing the rubric would be valuable for preparing presentations along expectations of fully developed components.

The overall consensus of the undergraduate teacher education students in the science methods course suggests the need to promote science literacy in the classroom with a technology component, together with other traditionally understood aspects of science literacy, such as the scientific method.

REFERENCES

Afflerbach, P. *Understanding and Using Reading Assessment*. Newark, DE: International Reading Association, 2007.

Alvermann, D., and C. McLean. "The Nature of Literacies." In *Secondary School Literacy: What Research Reveals for Classroom Practice*. Edited by L. Rush, A. J. Eakle, and A. Berger, 1–20. Urbana, IL: National Council of Teachers of English, 2007.

American Association for the Advancement of Science. "Project 2061 Science Benchmarks Online." 2009. http://www.project2061.org/.

Dodge, T., J. Jablon, and T. Bickart. *Constructing Curriculum for the Primary Grades*. Portland: Teaching Strategies Incorporated, 1994.

Dunston, P. J., and L. B. Gambrell. "Motivating Adolescent Learners to Read." In *Literacy Instruction for Adolescents: Research-Based Practice*, edited by K. D. Wood and W. E. Blanton, 269–286. New York: The Guilford Press, 2009.

Friedman, T. L. *The World is Flat: A Brief History of the Twenty-First Century*. New York: Farrar, Straus, and Giroux, 2005.

Hague, S. A., and G. E. Mason. "Using the Computer's Readability Measure to Teach Students to Revise Their Writing." *Journal of Reading*, 30, no. 1 (1986): 14–17.

Hull, G., and J. Zacher. "What is After-School Worth? Developing Literacy and Identity Out of School." *Voices in Urban Education* 3 (Winter/Spring 2004). Accessed December 23, 2009. http://www.annenberginstitute.org/VUE/spring04/Hull.php.

International Reading Association and National Council of Teachers of English. *Standards for the English Language Arts*. Newark, DE & Urbana, IL: NCTE and IRA, 1996.

McChesney, R. W. *Communication Revolution: Critical Junctures and the Future of Media*. New York: The New Press, 2007.

Messick, S. "Validity of Performance Assessment." In *Technical Issues in Large-Scale Performance Assessment*, edited by G. Phillips. Washington, DC: National Center for Educational Statistics, 1996.

Messick, S. "Validity of Test Interpretation and Use." In *Encyclopedia of Education Research*, edited by M. Alkin, 1487–1495. 6th ed. New York: Macmillan, 1992.

Mott, M. S., and M. A. Benus. "Digital Books with Media-Rich Paper: Enhancing Reading Comprehension through Touch User Interface." *Journal of Literacy and Technology* 7, no. 1 (2006). DOI: http://www.literacyandtechnology.org.

Mott, M. S., C. Etsler, and D. Drumgold. "Applying an Analytic Writing Rubric to Children's Hypermedia Narratives." *Early Childhood Research & Practice* 5, no. 1 (2003). DOI: http://ecrp.uiuc.edu/.

National Research Council. *National Science Education Standards*. Washington, DC: National Academy Press, 1996.

Nicol, D. J., and D. Macfarlane-Dick. "Formative Assessment and Self-Regulated Learning: A Model and Seven Principles of Good Feedback." *Studies in Higher Education,* 31, no. 2 (2006): 199–218.

Novak, J. R., J. L. Herman, and M. Gearhart. "Establishing Validity for Performance-Based Assessments: An Illustration for Collections of Student Writing." *Journal of Educational Research* 89, no. 4 (1996): 220–233. EJ 528 634.

Partnership for 21st Century Skills. *Learning for the 21st Century: A Report and MILE Guide for 21st Century Skills*. Washington, DC: Partnership for 21st Century Skill, 2003.

Prensky, M. "Digital Natives, Digital Immigrants." *On the Horizon* 9, no. 5 (2001). Retrieved http://www.marcprensky.com/writing/Prensky%20%20Digital%20Natives,%20Digital%20Immigrants%20-%20Part1.pdf

Sylvester, R., and W. Greenidge. "Digital Storytelling: Extending the Potential for Struggling Writers." *The Reading Teacher* 63, no. 4 (2009): 284–295.

Tierney, R. J., E. Bond, and J. Bresler. "Examining Literate Lives as Students Engage with Multiple Literacies." *Theory into Practice* 45 (2006): 359–367.

Yang, S. C. "A Dynamic Reading-Linking-to-Writing Model for Problem Solving within a Constructive Hypermedia Learning Environment." *Journal of Educational Multimedia and Hypermedia* 5, no. 3/4 (1996): 263–283.

CREDITS

Interactive Assessment Work-Map

1 START HERE

Directions

For the example assessment above you are now going to "interact" with it as you check off criteria and write brief statements and definitions about its general type and, specifically, its reliability, validity, value and utility technical characteristics. You are encouraged to infer how the assessment might be used in your own teaching if applicable.

2 How Is the Assessment Administered?

Individual ☐

Group ☐

3 Assessment, Test, Measurement, Evaluation Type

Note that an assessment can contain multiple types and/or degrees of type.

Test ☐ Achievement in what academic area/subject/domain?

Quiz ☐ For reinforcement/application or demonstrated understanding

Survey ☐ Cognitive and/or behavioral

Portfolio ☐ Collection of artifacts for learner demonstration of meeting various criteria and/or understanding

Inventory ☐ Collection of items/prompts for discernment of learning in a comprehensive manner, with all sub-elements of that area included

Artifact ☐ Specific evidence to learner demonstration of among various criteria and/or understanding

Exam ☐ Measuring specific content-area aligned to specific learning objectives

Case ☐ A specific unit of analysis or person with defined boundaries

Writing Prompt ☐ A query, question or directive to guide student writing

Content Area Performance/Presentation ☐

4 Reliability and Validity

Reliable ☐

Valid *FOR WHAT PURPOSE?*
Describe assessment features that support the validity type/s identification.

-Face ☐

-Content ☐

-Criterion-related ☐

-Construct ☐

-Concurrent ☐

-Predictive ☐

-Developmental ☐

5 Qualities and Characteristics

Check each box that applies and briefly notate how the assessment meets these defined criteria for assessment purpose, making inferences from results and interpreting data.

☐ Static- _____ Dynamic ☐

☐ Developmental

☐ Vertical

☐ Formative _____ Summative ☐

☐ Value for Who/When/How?

-Student ☐
-Teacher ☐
-Parent ☐
-Administrator ☐
-Community ☐

Utility ☐ (Leading to specific Actions)

Interactive Assessment Work-Map developed by M. Mott (2016).

Interactive Assessment Work-Map NOTES

6

Reliability and Validity Description

Reliable ☐

Valid *FOR WHAT PURPOSE?* Describe assessment features that support the validity type/s identification. See information on validity definitions in the *Reliability, Validity, Value, and Utility* section of this book.

-Face ☐

-Content ☐

-Criterion-related ☐

-Construct ☐

-Concurrent ☐

-Predictive ☐

-Developmental ☐

Interactive Assessment Work-Map developed by M. Mott (2016).

INFORMED TEACHING

Interactive Assessment Work-Map NOTES

Value and Utility

Discuss and describe the educational value of the assessment under review. What does it do? Who does it help and how? Why can it inform teaching and learning? Can it inform educational policy and leadership decision making? In what manner?

7

Value for …?

Students ☐
-Content Area
-Cognitive
-Social-Emotional

-Teachers ☐
-Inform Instruction
-Formative
-Summative
-Dynamic

Utility for …?

-Administrators ☐
-Support Supervision Goals and Policy
-Guide Schoolwide Efforts and Programming

-Parents and Community ☐
-Information for Parents on Status of Education

Interactive Assessment Work-Map developed by M. Mott (2016).

Interactive Assessment Work-Map NOTES

Applications to *Your* Professional Practice

8

Given the reliability, validity, value, and utility characteristics of the current assessment under review, discuss and describe how you would apply it in your professional practice. Hypothetically illustrate a reasoned use for the assessment and freely identify its strengths and limitations (validity issues) for making inferences from the results of the assessment for instruction.

Interactive Assessment Work-Map developed by M. Mott (2016).

ASSESSMENT EXAMPLE 7. CLASSROOM MANAGEMENT SURVEY SAMPLE

COLLECTING AND USING BEHAVIOR DATA IN CLASSROOMS

The use of data is not new to schools; however, reforms in education have emphasized the importance of setting high standards for all learners.[1] Data collection has never been as important as in the wake of the Every Student Succeeds Act (ESSA, 2015) which revised the No Child Left Behind Act (NCLB, 2001) and the American Recovery and Reinvestment Act (2009). Each of these revisions and laws have mandated systematic analysis of data collection to inform instructional decision making. Instructional decision making is a system of teaching and management practices (e.g., academic and behavioral) that uses data to inform and guide all instructional decisions. Basic foundations must be in place to facilitate data-driven decisions.

---

1 Stecker, Pamela M. Lembke, Erica S. Foeg. "Using progress-monitoring data to improve instructional decision making.(Report)", Preventing School Failure, Winter 2008 Issue.

INTRODUCTION TO POSITIVE BEHAVIOR INTERVENTION AND SUPPORT

Positive Behavior Intervention and Support (PBIS) is a framework designed to enhance discipline and behavior that promotes appropriate social behavior and increases learning. PBIS is a preventative, proactive, evidence-based, outcomes-focused, continuous, and multisystemic intervention that is used in schools (Scott and Barrett 2004; Sugai and Horner 2002, 2006). Additionally, PBIS is a systems-level approach to improving school climate through the use of proactive behavioral strategies (Horner, Sugai, Todd, and Lewis-Palmer 2005; Sprague and Horner 2007; Sugai and Horner 2002; Sugai et al. 2000). PBIS emphasizes the use of data for informing decisions at the school and classroom levels. Data indicate that when PBIS programming is implemented, there are functional, effective, efficient, and relevant behavioral improvements, including decreasing numbers of office discipline referrals (Metzler, Biglan, Rusby, and Sprague 2001; Nelson, Martella, and Garland 1998; Morrissey, Bohanon, and Fenning 2010; Taylor-Green and Kartub 2000; Rosenberg and Jackman 2003; Turnbull et al. 2002; Warren et al. 2003) and increased student learning.

PBIS is a framework in the application of Response to Intervention (RTI) principles for the improvement of social behavior outcomes through the combination of behavioral theory, behavior analysis, positive behavior supports, and prevention and implementation science. PBIS is an integrated implementation of behavior and academic supports (Sugai, Horner, Fixsen, and Blase 2010). It has been developed to improve how schools manage, organize, implement, and progress monitor behavioral practices in meeting the needs of all students (Sugai et al. 2000). Finally, PBIS is rooted in the person-centered values, where a team-based approach is used to consider an individual's needs and develop intervention strategies accordingly (Anderson and Freeman 2000; Carr et al.).

At the primary prevention level, also referred to as Universal Supports, PBIS is implemented with all students across all settings (Horner et al. 2009; Sugai and Horner 2002, 2006). Primary prevention is managed by a data-based decision-making team, which oversees the following critical features: (a) three to five positively stated expectations/rules, (b) procedures for teaching and modeling behavior expectations, (c) procedures for rewarding and/or acknowledging appropriate behaviors, (d) procedures for discouraging inappropriate behaviors, (e) ongoing assessment and problem analysis, and (f) plans for evaluation of outcomes and implementation using data-based decision making (George, Kincaid, and Polland-Sage 2009; Sugai and Horner 2002).

Nonresponders to primary prevention (also known as Tier 1) are accommodated in secondary (Tier 2) and tertiary (Tier 2) tiers of support (Horner et al. 2009; Sugai and Horner 2002, 2006). Usually, 10%–15% of students are in need of Tier 2 services that typically include small group settings for additional instruction (e.g., academic and behavior instruction) and increased progress monitoring. The Tier 3 level, or tertiary level, is individualized and intensive interventions. Four critical elements appear at all levels of PBIS: evidence-based practice, data-based decision making, systems-level implementation, and outcomes.

Good teaching is not about mimicking methods you were exposed to as a learner. It is about making informed decisions about methods of instruction that take into consideration your style of teaching, your students, and their instructional needs. Exploring the intersection between these three needs is an ongoing process through multiple data-collection methods of several components. Style of teaching includes some preliminary work understanding teacher, classroom management practices, and student behavior needs to be identified and addressed.

STYLE OF TEACHING
TEACHER CLASSROOM MANAGEMENT PRACTICES

Classroom management is the process by which teachers and schools create and maintain appropriate behavior of students in the classroom setting (Kratochwill, DeRoos, and Blair, n.d.). Support at the classroom level through understanding a teacher's classroom management style could be a contributing factor for the efficient and long-lasting implementation of PBIS. Effective teaching and learning cannot take place in an inadequately managed classroom. Effective teachers appear to be effective with students across the academic continuum regardless of the diversity in their classes. Effective teaching and learning cannot take place in a poorly managed classroom where there are no rules or procedures to guide classroom behavior. For teachers to make meaningful changes in classroom management styles involves gaining a better understanding of yourself. Making change in one's approach typically involves some sort of assessment. So what kind of classroom manager are you?

Understanding your classroom management profile will help increase your ability to address inappropriate social behavior before it escalates into something more serious. Furthermore, knowing your boundaries can potentially facilitate your interactions and ability to de-escalate potentially challenging conditions.

Table 7.1 What is your classroom management profile?[2]

	STRONGLY DISAGREE 1	DISAGREE 2	NEUTRAL 3	AGREE 4	STRONGLY AGREE 5
1. If a student is disruptive during class, I assign him/her to detention, without further discussion.					
2. I don't want to impose any rules on my students.					
3. The classroom must be quiet in order for students to learn.					
4. I am concerned about both what my students learn and how they learn.					
5. If a student turns in a late homework assignment, it is not my problem.					
6. I don't want to reprimand a student because it might hurt his/her feelings.					
7. Class preparation isn't worth the effort.					
8. I always try to explain the reasons behind my rules and decisions.					
9. I will not accept excuses from a student who is tardy.					
10. The emotional well-being of my students is more important than classroom control.					
11. My students understand that they can interrupt my lecture if they have a relevant question.					
12. If a student requests a hall pass, I always honor the request.					

---

2 Adapted from Santrock. http://education.indiana.edu/cas.

Take the short survey (Table 7.1) to determine your style or combination of styles. Table 7.1 and the instructions following are adaptations of parenting styles discussed in *Adolescence* by John T. Santrock. Each profile will be discussed after the survey.

Answer these twelve questions and learn more about your classroom management profile. The steps are simple:
- Read each statement carefully.
- Respond to each statement based upon either actual or imagined classroom experience. Check the corresponding box.
- Then, follow the scoring instructions below to score and learn your management style (See Table 7.1).

To score your quiz, add your responses:

Table 7.2

STATEMENTS	TOTAL SCORE	STYLE
1, 3, and 9		Authoritarian
4, 8, and 11		Authoritative
6, 10, and 12		Laissez-faire
2, 5, and 7		Indifferent

The purpose of this activity is for you to become familiar with your classroom management style and explore the different possible styles. Your own classroom management profile includes scores on each style that range from 3 to 15. Your strongest style preferences are indicated by the highest scores; however, it is likely that you will relate to characteristics of each style. Further, as you gain teaching experience, it is likely that your style will change. With experience, you will settle on a style that works best for you. In addition, you may find that you utilize different styles depending on the situation in which you find yourself. You may learn that different styles work best for you in different situations.

The *Authoritarian* teacher tends to be harsh, demanding, intolerant, autocratic, and punitive. This teacher uses a loud voice to gain student attention; s/he will demand compliance and very often assign seats for the entire year. The classroom environment is typically in straight rows with students completing independent activities, as conversation and group work are discouraged. The authoritarian teacher does not provide emotional support. Student anxiety is high and compliance is gained out of fear. The outcome of this classroom is distrust, and this management style does not produce behavioral change.

The *Authoritative* teacher tends to be firm but fair, making demands and imposing discipline in a caring atmosphere. This teacher uses effective strategies to gain student attention, all while maintaining high expectations in an emotionally supportive, positive, kind environment. The classroom environment is a collaborative working environment in which the teacher often provides explanations behind the processes, rules, and decisions. The authoritative teacher is emotionally supportive. The students trust and respect the teacher and feel safe in this classroom. The outcome for this classroom is positive growth and development, as the processes in place allow for more time to spend on the academic content and learning.

The *Indifferent* teacher tends to show no interest in their classrooms and or students. This teacher rarely demands anything, does not set limits, appears as though s/he has a detached personality, and is apathetic. The teacher may feel emotions ranging from helplessness to anger. The classroom environment is chaotic, and the teacher is bothered by the lack of effectiveness of his/her previous efforts. The indifferent teacher is not sympathetic. The students may be docile or belligerent, capable or slow learners. The outcome of this classroom is very little learning is happening. Behavior tends to increase across time, and warning signs can be missed for triggers of behavior.

The *Laissez-faire* teacher tends to be free-willing, with no limits. Student impulses and actions are accepted and not likely redirected or monitored. This teacher is affectionate, caring, and involved but tends to be extremely tolerant and exerts little or no control or discipline. This teacher strives to be liked and accepted by all students. The classroom environment is not conducive to constructive learning. The students report this is an easy teacher but state no learning is taking place. Students have a lack of trust in this laissez-faire teacher, as he or she is inconsistent in handling disruptive behavior. There are very few outcomes in this classroom, as it tends to be out of control, with lower expectations and motivation to achieve success.

Given that classroom management refers to all of what happens in the classroom (e.g., organization, space management, environment, time, and materials), teachers must effectively plan and prepare well as well as maximize student time on task. How one manages the classroom is the primary factor in how well your students achieve. Contrariwise, when students are successful and actively engaged in their work, they tend to be well-behaved. Therefore, keep students involved in their work, have students understand what is expected of them, maximize time on task, prevent confusion or disruption, and run a work environment but comfortable and enjoyable classroom. Remember that in the adult world, the workplace is one that is not always quiet; on the contrary, people continually collaborate, ask questions, inspire others, seek guidance, and so on.

In accepting the hypothesis that everything a teacher does in the classroom contributes to quality instruction and management, you cannot separate instruction and classroom management. When teachers apply their experience, teaching, communication mastery, skills and values, and caring, they empower and the students become an active part of the teacher/learning process.

CLASSROOM MANAGEMENT STRATEGIES

We understand, through research, that one of the classroom teacher's most important jobs is managing the classroom effectively. Teachers' actions in their classrooms have twice the impact on student achievement as do school policies regarding curriculum, assessment, staff collegiality, and community involvement (Marzano and Marzano 2003). Ineffective classroom management skills can waste instructional time, reduce time-on-task, and interrupt learning environments (Boyton and Boyton 2005; Vannest, Soares, and Harrison 2009; Vannest et al. 2010). Students cannot learn in a chaotic, poorly managed classroom, so take the following survey (Table 7.3) to help your understanding in how far along you are at mastering this important practice.

Table 7.3. Classroom Management Practice Survey

SURVEY QUESTIONS	RATING	
	YES	NO
1. I arrange my classroom to minimize crowding and distraction.		
2. I maximize structure and predictability in my classroom (e.g., explicit classroom routines, specific directions, systems, and process, etc.).		
3. I post, teach, review and reinforce 3–5 positively stated expectations (or rules).		
4. I provide more frequent acknowledgement for appropriate behaviors than inappropriate behaviors.		
5. I provide each student with multiple opportunities to respond and participate during instruction.		
6. My instruction actively engages students in observable ways (e.g., writing, verbalizing).		
7. I actively supervise my classroom (e.g., moving, scanning) during instruction.		
8. I ignore or provide quick, direct, explicit reprimands/redirections in response to inappropriate behavior.		
9. I have multiple strategies/systems in place to acknowledge appropriate behavior (e.g., token systems, class point systems, praise, etc.).		
10. In general, I provide specific feedback in response to social and academic behavior errors and correct responses.		
TOTAL		

Key:
Only look at the number of "yes" selections –

10–8	= Super
7–5	= So-So
>5	= Needs Improvement

Source: Adapted from Washburn, S. (2010) Center on Education and Lifelong Learning, Classroom Management Self Assessment. Revised Version: May 2010.

Sugai, G., Horner, R.H., & Todd, A.W. (2000). Effective behavior support: Self-assessment survey. Eugene: University of Oregon.

Sugai, G., Lewis-Palmer, T., Todd, A., & Horner, R.H. (2001). School-wide evaluation tool. Eugene: University of Oregon.

Sugai, G., and G. Colvin. Non-Classroom Management: Self-Assessment. University of Oregon: Office of Special Education Programs Center on Positive Behavioral Interventions and Supports, 2004.

Reinke, Wendy; Lewis-Palmer, Teri; and Merrell, Kenneth (2008). The Classroom Check-up: A Classwide Teacher Consultation Model for Increasing Praise and Decreasing Disruptive Behavior, School Psychology Review, 37(3): 315-332.

ASSESSMENT EXAMPLE 7. CLASSROOM MANAGEMENT SURVEY SAMPLE

Table 7.4. Teacher Assessment of Classroom Practices

	IMPLEMENT, MONITOR, & REVISE	IMPLEMENT, BUT INCONSISTENT	SOME ATTEMPT TO IMPLEMENT	DO NOT IMPLEMENT
	3	2	1	0
CLASSROOM MANAGEMENT				
I recognize positive student behavior four times more often than acknowledging student problematic behavior.				
Classroom rules are taught and managed in a positive way.				
Are transition procedures taught (e.g., entering and exiting the classroom and changing between activities)?				
The room is arranged and made assessable to all students and the teacher.				
Students have enrichment work after completing required work.				
I teach the allotted instructional time (e.g., bell to bell, review game if instruction is finished early).				
Instructional Management				
I ask questions that are clear and provide understandable directions for assignments.				
Does the daily schedule provide all students with varied activities (e.g., independent work, one-to-one instruction, small group, socialization, etc.)?				
Are the students actively engaged in the lesson?				
Instructional activities are linked to short-/long-term instructional goals.				
TEACHING TECHNIQUES				
Are the rules and consequences clear and consistent across all students?				
Do I provide verbal praise to the students?				
Is there a point system implemented in the classroom that includes diverse learners?				
Is feedback provided frequently (e.g., weekly)?				
CONSEQUENCE SYSTEM				
Are there predetermined consequences for rule violation implemented?				
Are the consequences delivered in a timely manner (e.g., day of incident)?				
Are students aware of their choices before escalation?				
Is there a strong family/school relationship?				

SCORING:

Table 7.5

AREA		ANSWER
Classroom Management	_____/6	
Instructional Management	_____/4	
Teaching Techniques	_____/4	
Consequence System	_____/4	

KEY:

3 = You consistently implement practices, monitor to ensure they are working, and make changes to improve.
2 = You implement practices, but you are inconsistent on which practices you deliver. This sends a mixed message to the students you teach.
1 = You attempt to implement some practices. This stage is typically where you see "new" teachers.
0 = You do not implement practices.

Adapted by D. Soares and L. Maxcy from Sugai, G., and G. Colvin. *Non-Classroom Management: Self-Assessment*. University of Oregon: Office of Special Education Programs Center on Positive Behavioral Interventions and Supports, 2004.

RULES AND OPERATING PROCEDURES

CLASSROOM ARRANGEMENT

The classroom, furniture and all, can be a powerful teaching tool. Fred Jones, classroom management expert and author of *Tools for Teaching*, explains: "A good classroom seating arrangement is the cheapest form of classroom management. It's discipline for free" (Dunbar and Villarruel 2004). The physical and social systems in classrooms are interwoven. The classroom environment has influence on the culture of the classroom, including learning, behavior, and teaching, so all classrooms should be arranged to facilitate positive collaborations.

ESTABLISHING RULES

Research on classroom management mostly focuses on rules and student codes of conduct. Researcher and professor Dr. David Schimmel (2003) states, "collaborative rule-making promotes mutual respect, cooperation, self-discipline, and personal responsibility while also providing the structure and security students need." By collaboratively setting rules and consequences, both teachers and students agree upon and understand the rules, thereby buying into the belief that students will support rules they establish. Best practice recommends minimizing the number of rules and ensuring they are direct, clear, and consistent as well as promoting positive behavior. Furthermore, teachers need to ensure that the rules are designed to support logical consequences for inappropriate behavior or rule breaking. These consequences should be explained in advance and should be related to the misbehavior so that students begin to connect the misbehavior with the consequence.

COLLECTING AND USING STUDENT BEHAVIOR DATA

Progress monitoring (PM) is common classroom practice and has been demonstrated to be an effective and efficient intervention for a variety of behaviors. Frameworks, such as PBIS and RTI, use progress monitoring as a formative process that assists teachers in assessing academic and behavior performance. PM involves repeated samples of student performance (e.g., daily or weekly tracking of a specific behavior). When this data is tracked and charted in a visual graph over time, it serves as a visual for decision making as well as providing students with consistent feedback on their performance (Vannest, Soares, Smith, and Williams 2012).

Issues and behaviors that respond to progress monitoring range from common school problems such as off-task and disruptive classroom behaviors to academic interventions and progress (Brookhart, Andolina, Zuza, and Furman 2004; Deno 2003; Ervin et al. 2007; Hosp and Donalson 2004; Sutherland, Palmer, Stichter, and Morgan 2008). Decades of research supports PM as a reliable and valid predictor of future performance on outcome measures (Deno 2003; Fuchs, Deno, and Mirkin 1984; Good and Jefferson 1998).

Fundamental components of progress monitoring include: (a) developing goals; (b) developing strategies to achieve goals; (c) monitoring progress towards goals; (d) reporting on progress towards goals; and (e) make changes as needed to keep making progress towards goals (Brown and Capp 2003; Deno 2003; Hosp and Donalson 2004).

DATA COLLECTION

STEP 1: IDENTIFY THE BEHAVIOR

Define a behavior that you wish to observe in specific, observable, and measurable terms. Be very specific, ensuring your definition is so narrow that other people could observe the described behavior. Use the following student surveys to determine specific student behavior that is in need of intervention.

Table 7.6 Student Self-Evaluation

	ALMOST ALWAYS	SOMETIMES	ALMOST NEVER
I listen when the teacher (or speaker) is talking.			
I follow directions the first time they are given.			
I am polite and respectful to students and adults.			
I ask for help when I don't understand.			
I raise my hand to answer questions in class.			
I do my best work.			
I turn in neat work and use my best handwriting.			
I finish my work on time.			

ASSESSMENT EXAMPLE 7. CLASSROOM MANAGEMENT SURVEY SAMPLE

Table 7.7 Student Behavior Checklist

	ALMOST ALWAYS	OFTEN	SOMETIMES	ALMOST NEVER
	3	2	1	0
UNDERSTANDING EMOTIONS				
The student recognizes others' body language (e.g., peers or teachers)				
The student is not aggressive toward:				
a. peers				
b. self				
c. authority				
The student empathizes with and is sympathetic to peers.				
The student uses different voice inflection when talking to peers and teachers.				
The student doesn't have any obvious intense fears or phobias.				
SELF-REGULATION				
The student handles emotion when upset or at a high energy level.				
Is the student involved in group activities?				
Can the student accept losing at a game?				
Can the student accept "no" for an answer?				
FLEXIBILITY				
Is the student able to take constructive criticism?				
Can the student accept consequences for his/her actions?				
Is unexpected change easily accepted?				
Does the student make an effort when things are difficult?				
Can the student ignore a situation that is unhealthy?				
PROBLEM SOLVING				
Can the student formulate a solution to a problem?				
Does the student introduce him/herself to someone new?				
Is the student able to pick up on nonverbal cues during conversation?				
Does the student wait before interjecting in a conversation?				
Does the student show remorse when apologizing?				
SOCIAL-EMOTIONAL BEHAVIORS				
Does the student join activities in appropriate ways?				
Does the student obey classroom rules?				
Does the student take turns during unstructured activities?				

*Adapted from *Elementary Social Skills Checklist*

SCORING:

Table 7.8

AREA		ANSWER
Understanding Emotion	_____/7	
Self-Regulation	_____/4	
Flexibility	_____/5	
Problem Solving	_____/5	
Social-Emotional Behaviors	_____/3	

Use the previous scores in determining deficit areas that should be written as individual goals for students.

STEP 2: OBSERVE AND RECORD DATA

There are many different methods for measuring behavior. Once we clearly define the behavior, we need to understand what we are going to observe and record data on. For example, if a student is exhibiting "tantrums" at school, we could measure numerous items:

- Number of tantrums during a period of time
- Length of tantrum
- After the triggering event, how long (latency) before the tantrum begins
- The total amount of time (percent) the student tantrums in a day
- The severity/intensity of the tantrum

Each of these pieces of data require different forms of measurement. In the table below, you will find a quick summary of some common data-collection methods to help you select the appropriate method. In Appendix A, you will find blank recording forms for each method.

Table 7.9 Selecting the Appropriate Behavior Collection Method

RECORDING METHOD	EXAMPLES	ADVANTAGES	DISADVANTAGES
Event/Frequency Recording is a simple counting of how many times a behavior occurs during a designated period of time.	Out of seat, shouting out, number of positive interactions with teacher	Easy Can take data while teaching Can translate into rate	Not helpful for very high rate behaviors or behaviors over extended periods of time
Interval Recording is used to measure the presence or absence of behavior within specific time intervals. You can use whole or partial interval recording.	Working on assignment, talking to peers, hitting	Can help identify patterns of behavior Can be translated to a percentage	Requires outside observer and undivided attention Provides estimate (less exact) Requires equal time periods
Momentary Time Sampling records the presence or absence of behaviors immediately following specified time intervals.	Every fifteen minutes, teacher looks to see if student is working on the assignment	Easy Estimate of occurrence	Does not capture how long the behavior is happening
Duration Recording records the total time or percentage of time that a behavior occurs within a specified time period.	Tantrums, sleeping, working on assignment, interacting with peer	Tells duration and frequency Can be translated to a percentage Works for high rate behaviors or difficult to event record	May require outside observer Use a stopwatch time instrument
Latency Recording is the measurement of the length of elapsed time between the onset of a stimulus and the occurrence of a behavior.	How long to start an assignment How long until student follows direction	Tells how long until behavior is initiated	Requires outside observer Use a stopwatch or time instrument

STEP 3: ESTABLISHING A BASELINE

To make change in behavior, it is important to know the prevalence of the problem. Baseline data is a measurement of the behavior taken before any interventions are implemented. This step is important, as it allows a teacher to make some comparisons of the behavior before and after implementation of an intervention. Baseline data should be stable prior to implementing an intervention. Baseline data that is stable typically would be represented by a flat line or a trend line that is parallel to the x-axis. However, when we are working with a behavior that is decreasing (decelerating trend line) and we want that behavior to be increasing (accelerating trend line), it is appropriate to intervene on the behavior that is decreasing in ordinate value. Likewise, when we are working with a behavior that is increasing (accelerating trend line) and we want that behavior to be decreasing (decelerating trend line), it is appropriate to intervene on the behavior that is increasing in ordinate value.

In some cases, the data may be highly variable and is it is difficult to determine the trend. In these cases, we can calculate the stability of the data. See the following example.

Follow these steps to calculate mean, range, and stability (See Table 7.10).

Table 7.10

DIRECTION	EXAMPLE
Find the mean of your data. To do this, add the values and divide by the number of data points.	For example, you have the data points of 4, 2, 5, 6, 8, 3, and 7. Adding these together equals 35. Then divide this total by the number of data points (in this case, 7). 35 divided by 7 gives you a mean of 5.
Calculate 50% of the mean. To do this, you divide the mean by 2.	In the preceding data, the mean was 5. Dividing this number by 2 equals 2.5.
Add the number that represents 50% of the mean to the mean.	In this example, that would be 5 (the mean) plus 2.5, equaling 7.5.
Subtract the number that represents 50% of the mean from the mean.	In this example, that would be 5 (the mean) minus 2.5, equaling 2.5.
You now have determined the range where all of your data points should fall to determine stability.	In this example, the established range of baseline data is 2.5–7.5

Going back to the original data points (4, 2, 5, 6, 8, 3, and 7), you notice that 2 falls outside this range and thus your data points do not represent stable baseline data (see the dotted line on the visual graph). The solution is to continue to collect baseline data until you can determine stability.

STEP 4: USING DATA TO MAKE EDUCATIONAL DECISIONS

The most effective way to summarize data for decision making is through a visual representation of the recorded data using a graph. Organizing data that you are collecting will assist in identifying patterns related to the observed behavior. As noted previously, baseline data is data that is observed and recorded prior to any interventions being implemented. Once an intervention is introduced and implemented, the data is referred to as intervention data. When using data to make decisions, you would make comparisons from the baseline to the intervention data to determine the outcome.

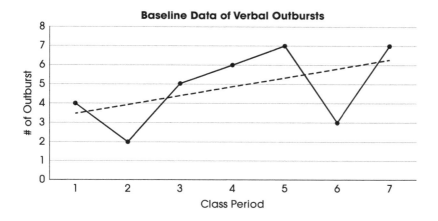

Figure 7.1

Baseline Data of Verbal Outbursts

VISUAL REPRESENTATION EXAMPLES

EXAMPLE 1:

Behavior: Shouting out in class (Figure 7.2)

Behavior Definition: Verbally disrupting the class by shouting out during class time instead of raising his hand.

Each time the student shouted out in class a tally mark was placed on the event recording sheet. This method is used to decrease verbal outbursts during Math.

Baseline: Baseline data was taken for seven days during Math. The students ranged anywhere from three verbal outbursts to five verbal outbursts.

Intervention: The intervention was implemented. Data was taken for an additional eight days. Verbal outbursts ranged from zero to two per math class.

Educational Decision: This intervention is working, and we would continue the intervention unless we see some changes in the progress monitoring.

EXAMPLE 2:

Behavior Definition: Being on task, as demonstrated by eye contact (e.g., looking at the teacher, looking at the assignment, or talking to the teacher about the appropriate topic).

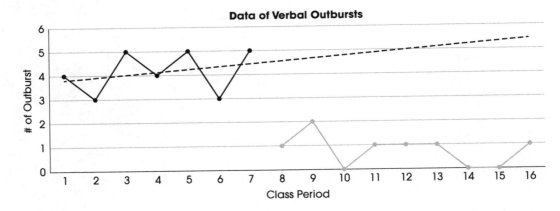

Figure 7.2

Total Observation Time: 10 min.   Length of each interval: 1 min.

DATE	INTERVAL #										TOTAL TIMES BEHAVIOR OCCURRED (✔)
3/25	1	2	3	4	5	6	7	8	9	10	
O OR ✔	O	✔	✔	✔	✔	O	O	O	O	O	4

The above interval data accounts for one data point (4). You would use the end column to graph the data.

Baseline: The baseline is stable with multiple data points. Data ranged from two to four. Intervention can begin.

Intervention: The intervention selected was to reinforce the on-task behavior each interval. The intervention was a verbal praise each time he is on task for the interval.

Educational Decision: This is a behavior we are trying to increase, so the intervention is working. We would continue with this intervention.

EXAMPLE 3:

Behavior Definition: Being on task, as demonstrated by eye contact (e.g., looking at the teacher, looking at the assignment, or talking to the teacher about the appropriate topic).

Total Observation Time: 10 min.   Length of each interval: 1 min.

DATE	INTERVAL #										TOTAL TIMES BEHAVIOR OCCURRED (✔)
3/25	1	2	3	4	5	6	7	8	9	10	
O OR ✔	O	✔	✔	✔	✔	O	O	O	O	O	4

ASSESSMENT EXAMPLE 7. CLASSROOM MANAGEMENT SURVEY SAMPLE

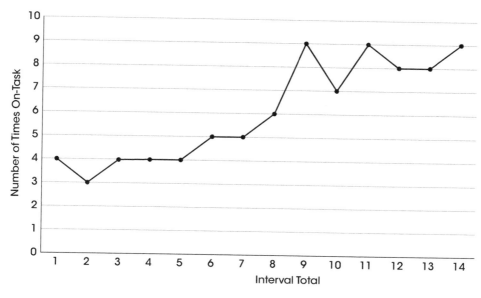

Figure 7.3

The above interval data accounts for one data point (4). You would use the end column to graph the data

This data so far is a replication of example 2. Now use this graph.

Series 1: Baseline

Series 2: Intervention 1 – Verbal Praise

Series 3: Intervention 2 – Sticker

Baseline: As in example 2, the baseline is stable, so we move to intervention.

Intervention 1: For this example, we evaluate the progress monitoring data for the first intervention. We do see some bounce; data ranges from three to five. The problem here is the intervention we are using, verbal praise, does not account for a big enough change in behavior.

Educational Decision 1: We need a stronger reinforcer, as verbal praise is not working.

Intervention 2: We begin to reinforce with a sticker each time the students is on task for the interval. Now we see data ranging from five to ten, but the data is in a positive trend line to the maximum number.

Educational Decision 2: The sticker is a stronger reinforcer and is working, so we continue to use the sticker.

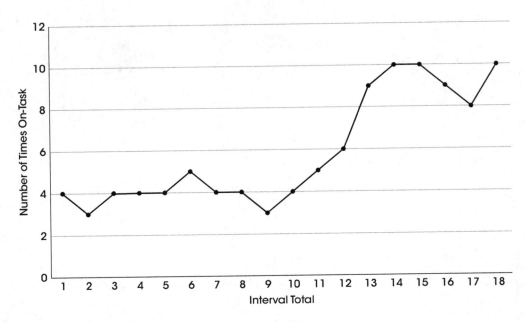

Figure 7.4

SUMMARY

Collecting and charting student behavior data helps teachers to: (a) better understand the purpose of and quantify the actual behavior; (b) guide in developing an intervention; (c) know if the intervention is having an impact on changing behavior.

APPENDIX A – DATA COLLECTION FORMS

EVENT RECORDING (FREQUENCY/TALLY COUNT) FORM

Student Name: _____   Observer: _____

Location: _____

Procedures:

- Write down the behavior that you will be looking for and its definition
- Every time you want to collect data:
  - Record the Date and Time
  - Make a tally mark every time that the behavior occurs (if the behavior does not occur, make sure to enter "0"–zero)
  - At the end of your observation period, total the number of tally marks for that day (if using a different method to keep track of behavior, enter the total in the Total column). (This is what you graph.)

Behavior Definition (in specific, observable, measurable terms):
_____
_____

Source: Adapted from Kansas Institute for Positive Behavior Support. (2012)
pbismissouri.org/wp-content/uploads/2017/06/7.1-Event-Recording-Form-1.docx

Table AA.1

DATE	TIME	TALLY EVERY TIME THAT THE BEHAVIOR OCCURS	TOTAL NUMBER OF TIMES BEHAVIOR OCCURRED

INTERVAL RECORDING FORM

Student Name: _____

Observer: _____

Subject: _____

Behavior Definition (in specific, observable, measurable terms):

_____

_____

Total Observation Time: _____

Length of each interval: _____

DATE	INTERVAL #										TOTAL TIMES BEHAVIOR OCCURRED (✔)
	1	2	3	4	5	6	7	8	9	10	
O OR ✔											

DATE	INTERVAL #										TOTAL TIMES BEHAVIOR OCCURRED (✔)
	1	2	3	4	5	6	7	8	9	10	
O OR ✔											

DATE	INTERVAL #										TOTAL TIMES BEHAVIOR OCCURRED (✔)
	1	2	3	4	5	6	7	8	9	10	
O OR ✔											

LATENCY RECORDING FORM

Student Name: _____   Observer: _____

Subject: _____

Behavior Definition (in specific, observable, measurable terms):
_____
_____

DATE	ENTER TIME WHEN THE INSTRUCTION IS GIVEN	ENTER TIME WHEN BEHAVIOR STARTS	MINUTES FOR THE BEHAVIOR TO BEGIN

REFERENCES

American Recovery and Reinvestment Act of 2009, Public Law No. 111-5 (2009). http://www.gpo.gov/fdsys/pkg/PLAW-111publ5/pdf/PLAW-111publ5.pdf.

Anderson, C. M., and K. A. Freeman, K. A. "Positive Behavior Support: Expanding the Application of Applied Behavior Analysis." *The Behavior Analyst* 23, no. 1 (2000): 85.

Brookhart, S. M., M. Andolina, M. Zuza, and R. Furman. "Minute Math: An Action Research Study of Student Self-Assessment." *Educational Studies in Mathematics* 57, no. 2 (2004): 213–227.

Brown, K., and R. Capp. "Better Data for Better Learning." *Leadership* 33, no, 2 (2003): 18.

Carr, E. G., G. Dunlap, R. H. Horner, R. L. Koegel, A. P. Turnbull, and W. Sailor. "Positive Behavior Support: Evolution of an Applied Science." *Journal of Positive Behavior Interventions* 4 (2002): 4–16.

Deno, S. L. (2003). "Developments in Curriculum-Based Measurement." *Journal of Special Education* 37, no. 3 (2003): 184–192.

Dunbar, C., and F. A. Villarruel. "What a Difference the Community Makes: Zero Tolerance Policy Interpretation and Implementation." *Equity & Excellence in Education* 37, no. 4 (2004): 351–359.

Ervin, R. A., Schaughency, E., Matthews, A., Goodman, S. D., & McGlinchey, M. T. (2007). Primary and secondary prevention of behavior difficulties: Developing a data-informed problem-solving model to guide decision making at a school-wide level. *Psychology in the Schools, 44*(1), 7-18. Every Student Succeeds Act of 2015, Public Law 114-95 (2015). https://www.ed.gov/essa?src=rn

Fuchs, L. S., S. L. Deno, and P. K. Mirkin. "The Effects of Frequent Curriculum-Based Measurement and Evaluation on Pedagogy, Student Achievement, and Student Awareness of Learning." *American Educational Research Journal* 21, no. 2 (1984): 449–460.

George, H. P., D. Kincaid, and J. Polland-Sage. "Primary Tier Interventions and Supports." In *Handbook of Positive Behavior Support*, edited by W. Sailor, G. Dunlop, G. Sugai, and R. Horner, 375–394. New York, NY: Springer, 2009.

Good, R., and G. Jefferson. "Contemporary Perspectives on Curriculum-Based Measurement Validity." In *Advanced Applications of Curriculum-Based Measurement*, edited by M. R. Shinn, 61–88. New York, NY: Guilford, 1998.

Horner, R. H., Sugai, G., Todd, A. W., & Lewis-Palmer, T. "Schoolwide Positive Behavior Support." In Linda M. Bambara and Lee Kern, *Individualized Supports for Students with Problem Behaviors: Designing Positive Behavior Plans*, 359–390. New York: Guilford Press, 2005.

Horner, R., G. Sugai, K. Smolkowski, L. Eber, J. Nakasato, A. Todd, and J. Esperanza. "A Randomized, Wait-List Controlled Effectiveness Trial Assessing School-Wide Positive Behavior Support in Elementary Schools." *Journal of Positive Behavior Interventions* 11 (2009): 133–145.

Hosp, W., & Donaldson, W., (Nov. 2004). National Center on Student Progress Monitoring: What Progress Monitoring can do for You. Retrieved from http://www.studentprogress.org/library/Presentations/WhatProgressMonitoring.pdf.

Kratochwill, T. K., R. DeRoos, and S. Blair. *Classroom. Management Modules*. Washington, DC: American Psychological Association, n.d. http://www.apa.org/education/k12/classroom-mgmt.aspx

Metzler, C. W., A. Biglan, J. C. Rusby, and J. R. Sprague. "Evaluation of a Comprehensive Behavior Management Program to Improve School-Wide Positive Behavior Support." *Education and Treatment of Children* 24, no. 4 (November 2001): 448–479.

Morrissey, K. L., H. Bohanon, and P. Fenning. "Positive Behavior Support Teaching and Acknowledging Expected Behaviors in an Urban High School." *Teaching Exceptional Children* 42, no. 5 (2010): 26–35.

Nelson, J. R., R. Martella, and B. Galand. "The Effects of Teaching School Expectations and Establishing a Consistent Consequence on Formal Office Disciplinary Actions." *Journal of Emotional and Behavioral Disorders* 6, no. 3 (1998): 153–161.

No Child Left Behind Act of 2001, Public Law No. 107-110 (2001). http://www.gpo.gov/fdsys/pkg/PLAW-107publ110/pdf/PLAW-107publ110.pdf

Rosenberg, M. S., and L. A. Jackman. "Development, Implementation, and Sustainability of Comprehensive School-Wide Behavior Management Systems." *Intervention in School and Clinic* 39, no. 1 (2003): 10–21.

Schimmel, D. M. (2003). Collaborative rule-making and citizenship education: An antidote to the undemocratic hidden curriculum. *American Secondary Education*, 16–35.

Scott, T. M., and S. B. Barrett. "Using Staff and Student Time Engaged in Disciplinary Procedures to Evaluate the Impact of School-Wide PBS." *Journal of Positive Behavior Interventions* 6, no. 1 (2004): 21–27.

Sugai, G., and R. Horner. "The Evolution of Discipline Practices: School-Wide Positive Behavior Supports." *Child & Family Behavior Therapy* 24, no. 1–2 (2002): 23–50.

Sugai, G., and R. H. Horner. "Introduction to the Special Series on Positive Behavior Support in Schools." *Journal of Emotional and Behavioral Disorders* 10, no. 3 (2002): 130.

Sugai, G., and R. R. Horner. "A Promising Approach for Expanding and Sustaining School-Wide Positive Behavior Support." *School Psychology Review* 35, no. 2 (2006): 245.

Sugai, G., R. H. Horner, D. Fixsen, and K. Blase. "Developing Systems-Level Capacity for RTI Implementation: Current Efforts and Future Directions." In *Response to Intervention: Empowering All Students to Learn: A Critical Account of the Science and Practice*, edited by T. A. Glover and S. Vaughn, 286–309. New York: Guilford Press, 2010.

Sutherland, K. S., T. Lewis-Palmer, J. Stichter, and P. L. Morgan. "Examining the Influence of Teacher Behavior and Classroom Context on the Behavioral and Academic Outcomes for Students with Emotional or Behavioral Disorders." *The Journal of Special Education* 41, no. 4 (2008): 223–233.

Taylor-Green, S. J., and D. T. Kartub. "Durable Implementation of School-Wide Behavior Support: The High Five Program." *Journal of Positive Behavior Interventions* 2, no. 4 (2000): 233.

Turnbull, A., H. Edmonson, P. Griggs, D. Wickham, W. Sailor, R. Freeman, and L. Riffel. "A Blueprint for Schoolwide Positive Behavior Support: Implementation of Three Components." *Exceptional Children* 68, no, 3 (2002): 377–402.

Vannest, K.J., D. A. Soares, J. R. Harrison, L. Brown, and R. I. Parker. "Changing Teacher Time." *Preventing School Failure* 54, no. 2 (2010): 86–98. doi: 10.1080/10459880903217739.

Vannest, K.J., D. A. Soares, and J. R. Harrison. "Changing Teacher Time Use through Goal Setting, Performance Feedback and Self-Monitoring." *Preventing School Failure* 18, no. 3 (2009): 33–39.

Vannest, K. J., D. A. Soares, S. L. Smith, and L. E. Williams. "Progress Monitoring to Support Science Learning for All Students." *Teaching Exceptional Children* 44, no. 6 (2012): 66–72.

CREDITS

Interactive Assessment Work-Map

Directions

For the example assessment above you are now going to "interact" with it as you check off criteria and write brief statements and definitions about its general type and, specifically, its reliability, validity, value and utility technical characteristics. You are encouraged to infer how the assessment might be used in your own teaching if applicable.

START HERE

1

2 🖊️

How Is the Assessment Administered?

Individual ☐
Group ☐

3

Assessment, Test, Measurement, Evaluation Type

Note that an assessment can contain multiple types and/or degrees of type.

Test ☐ Achievement in what academic area/subject/domain?

Quiz ☐ For reinforcement/application or demonstrated understanding

Survey ☐ Cognitive and/or behavioral

Portfolio ☐ Collection of artifacts for learner demonstration of meeting various criteria and/or understanding

Inventory ☐ Collection of items/prompts for discernment of learning in a comprehensive manner, with all sub-elements of that area included

Artifact ☐ Specific evidence to learner demonstration of among various criteria and/or understanding

Exam ☐ Measuring specific content-area aligned to specific learning objectives

Case ☐ A specific unit of analysis or person with defined boundaries

Writing Prompt ☐ A query, question or directive to guide student writing

Content Area Performance/Presentation ☐

Qualities and Characteristics

Check each box that applies and briefly notate how the assessment meets these defined criteria for assessment purpose, making inferences from results and interpreting data.

☐ Static- _____ Dynamic ☐
☐ Developmental
☐ Vertical
☐ Formative _____ Summative ☐
☐ Value for Who/When/How?
 -Student ☐
 -Teacher ☐
 -Parent ☐
 -Administrator ☐
 -Community ☐
 Utility ☐ (Leading to specific Actions) _____

5

4

Reliability and Validity

Reliable ☐

Valid *FOR WHAT PURPOSE?*
Describe assessment features that support the validity type/s identification.

-Face ☐
-Content ☐
-Criterion-related ☐
-Construct ☐
-Concurrent ☐
-Predictive ☐
-Developmental ☐

Interactive Assessment Work-Map developed by M. Mott (2016).

Interactive Assessment Work-Map NOTES

6

Reliability and Validity Description

Reliable ☐

Valid **FOR WHAT PURPOSE?** *Describe assessment features that support the validity type/s identification. See information on validity definitions in the Reliability, Validity, Value, and Utility section of this book.*

-Face ☐

-Content ☐

-Criterion-related ☐

-Construct ☐

-Concurrent ☐

-Predictive ☐

-Developmental ☐

Interactive Assessment Work-Map developed by M. Mott (2016).

Interactive Assessment Work-Map NOTES

Value and Utility

Discuss and describe the educational value of the assessment under review. What does it do? Who does it help and how? Why can it inform teaching and learning? Can it inform educational policy and leadership decision making? In what manner?

7

Value for ...?

Students ☐
-Content Area
-Cognitive
-Social-Emotional

-Teachers ☐
-Inform Instruction
-Formative
-Summative
-Dynamic

Utility for ...?

-Administrators ☐
-Support Supervision Goals and Policy
-Guide Schoolwide Efforts and Programming
-Parents and Community ☐
-Information for Parents on Status of Education

Interactive Assessment Work-Map developed by M. Mott (2016).

Interactive Assessment Work-Map NOTES

Applications to *Your Professional Practice*

8

Given the reliability, validity, value, and utility characteristics of the current assessment under review, discuss and describe how you would apply it in your professional practice. Hypothetically illustrate a reasoned use for the assessment and freely identify its strengths and limitations (validity issues) for making inferences from the results of the assessment for instruction.

Interactive Assessment Work-Map developed by M. Mott (2016).

ASSESSMENT EXAMPLE 8. NORM-REFERENCE ACHIEVEMENT TEST DATA

NORM-REFERENCE TESTS

Norm-Reference Tests are standardized tests designed to rank and compare students. Norm-reference tests yield standard test scores, which provide educators with data to compare one student's skills to others in the same classroom, grade level, or age group nationally. Therefore, classroom teachers, principals, and district personnel can use the information to assist in measuring students' abilities, to compare one student's achievement to others, and/or to evaluate the effectiveness of teaching and programs.

More often, teachers use norm-reference test scores to better understand how one student's performance in their classroom compares to other students' performance. For example, consider the STAR Reading Assessment given to a group of third-grade students. Ms. Alef teaches reading and language arts to twenty-one third-grade students (Figure 8.1). She administers the STAR Reading Assessment to her students on August 27 to determine their reading scale score. See Figure 8.1, which represents the scaled score for each student in her classroom.

Table 8.1

CATEGORY/LEVELS	CURRENT BENCHMARK	NUMBER/PERCENT	BENCHMARK FOR STATE ASSESSMENT
PROFICIENT			
Level 5	At/Above 815 SS	0/0%	At/Above 924 SS
Level 4	At/Above 405 SS	8/	At/Above 514 SS
LESS THAN PROFICIENT			
Level 3	Below 404 SS	5/	Below 514 SS
Level 2	Below 296 SS	2/	Below 413 SS
Level 1	Below 181 SS	6/	Below 304
STUDENTS TESTED		**21**	

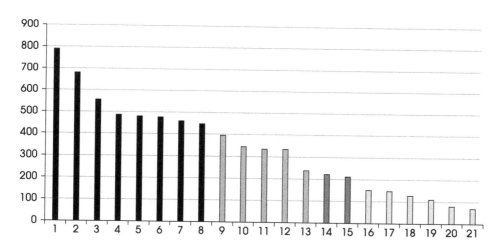

Figure 8.1

STAR Assessment Data. Student #1 had the highest scale score of 790, while student #21 had the lowest scale score of 85. The graph represents two basic forms of data: the individual scale score for each student and the level of proficiency.

UNDERSTANDING THE DATA

When Ms. Alef looks at the data chart, it is important that she understands not only the overall classroom information but also the scale score for each student and the additional information provided in the data report. The individual student information will later assist the teacher with meeting the instructional and learning needs of her students.

Ms. Alef notes that none of her students scored high enough on this administration to be classified as level 5 Proficient; however, eight of her students scored a Level 4 proficient. In other words, when comparing the skills needed to demonstrate proficiency, eight out of twenty-one students demonstrated proficiency on the skills being measured. For a deeper understanding of the data, the teacher examines each student's individual report.

INDIVIDUAL STUDENT REPORTS

John is one of the students whose scale score fell in the proficient category Level 4. On close examination of his individual report, the teacher notes the following:

Table 8.2

STAR READING SCORES: JOHN	
SS: 790 (Scaled Score)	John's Scaled Score is based on the difficulty of the questions and the number of correct responses.
PR: 98 (Percentile Rank)	John scored greater than 98% of students nationally in the same grade.
GE: 7.0 (Grade Equivalent)	John's test performance is better than that of an average seventh grader after the start of the school year.
IRL: 6.3 (Instructional Reading Level)	John would be best served by instructional materials prepared at the sixth-grade level.
Est. ORF: 170 Estimated Oral Reading Fluency	John can likely read 170 words per minute correctly on grade-level-appropriate text.
DOMAIN SCORES	
	Domain scores, ranging from 0–100, estimate John's percent of mastery on skills in each domain at a third-grade level.
READING RECOMMENDATION	
ZPD: 4.3–7.0 (Zone of Proximal Development	John's ZPD identifies books at the right level to provide optimal reading challenge without frustration.

Lynda is one of the students whose scaled score fell in the less than proficient category Level 1. On close examination of her individual report, the teacher notes the following:

STAR READING SCORES: LYNDA	
SS: 110 (Scaled Score) Level 1	Lynda's Scaled Score is based on the difficulty of the questions and the number of correct responses.
PR: 4 (Percentile Rank)	Lynda scored greater than 4% of students nationally in the same grade.
GE: 1.5 (Grade Equivalent)	Lynda's test performance is comparable to that of an average first grader after the fifth month of the school year.
IRL: PP (Instructional Reading Level)	Lynda would be best served by instructional materials prepared at the pre-kindergarten level.
Est. ORF: 35 Estimated Oral Reading Fluency	Lynda can likely read 35 words per minute correctly on grade-level-appropriate text.

DOMAIN SCORES	
	Domain scores, ranging from 0–100, estimate Lynda's percent of mastery on skills in each domain at a third-grade level.

Reading Recommendation

ZPD: 1.5–2.5 (Zone of Proximal Development	Lynda's ZPD identifies books at the right level to provide optimal reading challenge without frustration.

When looking at the individualized reports for each student, the teacher gains valuable information regarding how each student compares to his/her peers in each category. Norm-reference tests provide the type of information allowing educators to rank their students and to compare their achievement to others.

PRINCIPAL AND SUPERINTENDENT DATA ANALYSIS FROM LARGE-SCALE NORM-REFERENCE DATA

Norm-reference tests provide information about patterns of groups along test content, criteria, or construct. Large-scale testing leads to high utility for making inferences from results about the tested groups. For example, a superintendent might see STAR reading results in Spanish for third-grade students in a larger urban school system. One group of students scores much higher than another. Are the two groups in different programs? Let's say that one group was placed in a bilingual setting and the other group across town in a pull-out language enrichment curriculum. The utility of a measure is that degree to which inferences can be trusted and are valid for decisions about large groups of people. In this case, the superintendent can evaluate educational programming affecting hundreds or thousands of students in order to relocate funds to more effectively meet the needs of groups of students, based upon the data. A classroom assessment, providing information for a teacher to increase the educational specificity of her objectives, accomplishes a different task. Thus, different assessments meet the needs of different constituents in the educational community.

ASSESSMENT EXAMPLE 8. NORM-REFERENCE ACHIEVEMENT TEST DATA

Interactive Assessment Work-Map

Directions

For the example assessment above you are now going to "interact" with it as you check off criteria and write brief statements and definitions about its general type and, specifically, its reliability, validity, value and utility technical characteristics. You are encouraged to infer how the assessment might be used in your own teaching if applicable.

START HERE

1

How Is the Assessment Administered?

Individual ☐

Group ☐

2 🖊

3

Assessment, Test, Measurement, Evaluation Type

Note that an assessment can contain multiple types and/or degrees of type.

Test ☐ Achievement in what academic area/subject/domain? _____

Quiz ☐ For reinforcement/application or demonstrated understanding _____

Survey ☐ Cognitive and/or behavioral _____

Portfolio ☐ Collection of artifacts for learner demonstration of meeting various criteria and/or understanding _____

Inventory ☐ Collection of items/prompts for discernment of learning in a comprehensive manner, with all sub-elements of that area included _____

Artifact ☐ Specific evidence to learner demonstration of among various criteria and/or understanding _____

Exam ☐ Measuring specific content-area aligned to specific learning objectives _____

Case ☐ A specific unit of analysis or person with defined boundaries _____

Writing Prompt ☐ A query, question or directive to guide student writing _____

Content Area Performance/Presentation ☐ _____

Qualities and Characteristics

Check each box that applies and briefly notate how the assessment meets these defined criteria for assessment purpose, making inferences from results and interpreting data.

☐ Static- _____ Dynamic ☐

☐ Developmental

☐ Vertical

☐ Formative _____ Summative ☐

☐ Value for Who/When/How?

-Student ☐
-Teacher ☐
-Parent ☐
-Administrator ☐
-Community ☐

Utility ☐ (Leading to specific Actions) _____

5

Reliability and Validity

Reliable ☐

Valid *FOR WHAT PURPOSE?*
Describe assessment features that support the validity type/s identification.

-Face ☐

-Content ☐

-Criterion-related ☐

-Construct ☐

-Concurrent ☐

-Predictive ☐

-Developmental ☐

4

Interactive Assessment Work-Map developed by M. Mott (2016).

Interactive Assessment Work-Map NOTES

6

Reliability and Validity Description

Reliable ☐

Valid **_FOR WHAT PURPOSE?_** *Describe assessment features that support the validity type/s identification. See information on validity definitions in the Reliability, Validity, Value, and Utility section of this book.*

-Face ☐

-Content ☐

-Criterion-related ☐

-Construct ☐

-Concurrent ☐

-Predictive ☐

-Developmental ☐

Interactive Assessment Work-Map developed by M. Mott (2016).

Interactive Assessment Work-Map NOTES

Value and Utility

Discuss and describe the educational value of the assessment under review. What does it do? Who does it help and how? Why can it inform teaching and learning? Can it inform educational policy and leadership decision making? In what manner?

7

Value for ...?

Students ☐
-Content Area
-Cognitive
-Social-Emotional
-Teachers ☐
-Inform Instruction
-Formative
-Summative
-Dynamic

Utility for ...?

-Administrators ☐
-Support Supervision Goals and Policy
-Guide Schoolwide Efforts and Programming
-Parents and Community ☐
-Information for Parents on Status of Education

Interactive Assessment Work-Map developed by M. Mott (2016).

Interactive Assessment Work-Map NOTES

Applications to *Your Professional Practice*

8

Given the reliability, validity, value, and utility characteristics of the current assessment under review, discuss and describe how you would apply it in your professional practice. Hypothetically illustrate a reasoned use for the assessment and freely identify its strengths and limitations (validity issues) for making inferences from the results of the assessment for instruction.

Interactive Assessment Work-Map developed by M. Mott (2016).

CPSIA information can be obtained
at www.ICGtesting.com
Printed in the USA
LVHW05s0953210818
587538LV00001B/24/P